EARLY-CHRISTIAN EPITAPHS
FROM ANATOLIA

Society of Biblical Literature

TEXTS AND TRANSLATIONS
EARLY CHRISTIAN LITERATURE SERIES

edited by
Harold W. Attridge

Texts and Translations 35
Early Christian Literature Series 8

EARLY-CHRISTIAN EPITAPHS
FROM ANATOLIA

EARLY-CHRISTIAN EPITAPHS
FROM ANATOLIA

by
Gary J. Johnson

Scholars Press
Atlanta, Georgia

EARLY-CHRISTIAN EPITAPHS
FROM ANATOLIA

by

Gary J. Johnson

© 1995
Society of Biblical Literature

Library of Congress Cataloging-in-Publication Data
Johnson, Gary J.
    Early-Christian epitaphs from Anatolia / by Gary J. Johnson.
      p.   cm. — (Texts and translations ; no. 35. Early Christian
    literature series ; 8)
    Includes bibliographical references and indexes.
    ISBN 0-7885-0120-8 (alk. paper).
      1. Christianity—Turkey—Early church, ca. 30-600—Sources.
    2. Turkey—Church history—Sources. 3. Epitaphs—Turkey.
    4. Inscriptions, Greek—Turkey. I. Title. II. Series: Texts and
    translation ; 35. III. Series: Texts and translations Early Christian
    literature series ; 8.
    BR1080.J64   1995
    275.61'01—dc20   94-40061
                                                CIP

ISBN 1-58983-143-8 (pbk.-alk.paper)

Printed in the United States of America
on acid-free paper

This work is dedicated to

BONNIE RUTH		LOIS
LANGSTON	and	HUGHES
ROGERS		BECKWITH

my grandmother   my mother-in-law

who died

18 April 1993   17 April 1993

and sleep easy in their faith

Young County, Texas   Albemarle County, Virginia

TABLE OF CONTENTS

ACKNOWLEDGMENTS

The idea of preparing this volume came from Prof. Robert L. Wilken. The format was devised in consultation with Prof. Wilken and Prof. William R. Schoedel. The final product has been significantly improved by the advice of Dean Harold W. Attridge and the anonymous reviewers.

Completion of the project was aided by the efforts of several excellent typists at three different institutions: Nancy Jordan (University of Richmond, VA), Janet Rose (University of Michigan), Robin Day and Patricia Finn (University of Southern Maine); and by the efficiency of Adrienne Andrews, Interlibrary Loan Assistant of the University of Southern Maine.

The work began in a library carrel loaned to me by R. Bruce Hitchner, and only was finished with the aid of a computer and software provided by Deans Richard G. Stebbins and Julien S. Murphy of the University of Southern Maine. I am grateful to all of these individuals for their help.

In addition, I owe a special debt to my wife and sons for their unfailing support: Lois, Quinton, Julian, Allen. Thanks!

ABBREVIATIONS and SHORT TITLES

AS   = *Anatolian Studies*

BCH   = *Bulletin de Correspondance Hellénique*

BJRL   = *Bulletin of the John Rylands Library*

Calder, "Early Christian Epitaphs" = W.M. Calder, "Early-Christian
       Epitaphs from Phrygia," *AS* 5 (1955)

Calder, "The Epigraphy of the Anatolian Heresies" = W.M. Calder, "The
       Epigraphy of the Anatolian Heresies," in *Anatolian Studies
       Presented to Sir William Mitchell Ramsay* (Manchester:
       Manchester University Press, 1923)

CIG   = *Corpus Inscriptionum Graecarum*

CRAI   = *Comptes rendues de l'Académie des inscriptions et belles-
       lettres*

Gibson, *CFC* = Elsa Gibson, *The "Christians For Christians" Inscriptions
       of Phrygia* (Harvard Theological Studies 32; Missoula, MT:
       Scholars Press, 1978)

IGR   = *Inscriptiones Graecae ad Res Romanas Pertinentes*

JRS   = *Journal of Roman Studies*

Kubinska, *Les Monuments* = Jadwiga Kubinska, *Les Monuments funéraires
       dans les Inscriptions grecques de l'Asie mineure* (Warsaw:
       Center for Mediterranean Archeology, Polish Academy of
       Sciences, 1968)

MAMA   = *Monumenta Asiae Minoris Antiqua* (8 vols., Manchester:
       Manchester University Press, 1928-1962); vol.9 = *Journal of
       Roman Studies Monographs* 4 (1988)

NewDocs   = G.H.R. Horsley (ed., vols.1-5); S.R. Llewelyn and R.A.
       Kearsley (eds., vol. 6), *New Documents Illustrating Early
       Christianity* (North Ryde, N.S.W., Australia: Macquarie
       University, 1981-1992)

Ramsay, *CB* = W.M. Ramsay, *The Cities and Bishoprics of Phrygia* (2
       vols.; Oxford: Clarendon, 1895-97)

Şahin, *Iznik* = Sencer Şahin, *Katalog der Antiken Inschriften des Museums von Iznik (Nikaia)* (vols. 1, 2.1, 2.2, 2.3, Bonn: Rudolf Habelt, 1979-1987)

SBBerlin = *Sitzungberichte der Preussischen Akademie der Wissenschaften*

Sheppard, "Jews, Christians, and Heretics" = A.R.R. Sheppard, "Jews, Christians, and Heretics in Acmonia and Eumeneia," *AS* 29 (1979) 173

TAM = *Tituli Asiae Minoris* (4 vols.; Vienna: Österreichischen Akademie der Wissenschaften, 1901-1978)

ANATOLIAN SITES

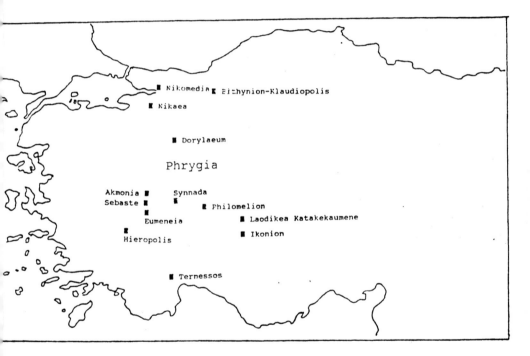

Nikomedia Bithynion-Klaudiopolis

Nikaea

Dorylaeum

Phrygia

Akmonia Synnada
Sebaste   Philomelion

Eumeneia   Laodikea Katakekaumene

Hieropolis   Ikonion

Termessos

Χρηστιανοὶ
Χρηστιανοῖς

Αὐρ(ήλιος) Πατρίκις κὲ Μακεδόν-
ις κὲ Ζωτικὸς κὲ Αμμιας κὲ 'Ε-
πικτὴς γνησίῳ πατρὶ Κυρίλλῳ κὲ μητρὶ Αμμια κὲ υἱοῖς
'Ονησίμῳ κὲ Κυρίλλῳ κὲ Πα-
τρικίῳ κὲ ἀδελφῇ Δόμνῃ
μνήμης χάριν.

Christians
for Christians

Aurelios Patrikis and Makedonis
and Zotikos and Ammias and
Epiktes (dedicated this) for (their) dear father,
Kyrillos, and (their) mother, Ammia, and for
(their) sons, Onesimos and Kyrillos and
Patrikios, and for (their) sister, Domna; in
memory.

This photograph was published originally as Plate 19 in Elsa Gibson, *The "Christians for Christians" Inscriptions of Phrygia* (Harvard Theological Studies 32; Missoula, MT: Scholars Press, 1978), copyright 1978 by the President and Fellows of Harvard College. Reprinted by permission.

INTRODUCTION

This book is a collection of early-Christian funerary inscriptions/epitaphs from Anatolia (modern Turkey). The majority of the epitaphs are from central Anatolia, particularly the ancient regions of Phrygia and Bithynia. Chapter 1, for the purpose of comparison, offers a small sample of more or less typical, non-Christian epitaphs from the same territory. Most of the epitaphs date approximately from the period C.E. 250-350. Altogether, the early-Christian epitaphs of Anatolia constitute a significant, but often overlooked source of information about the history and nature of the Early Church. This significance is underscored by the wider prominence of Anatolia as one of the earliest strongholds of the Christian movement.

Epitaphs long have been regarded as an irreplaceable asset by historians of Greece and Rome. Among other uses, they allow us to glimpse (however briefly) something of the lives and attitudes of the average and otherwise unknown inhabitants of the ancient Mediterranean world. To a large degree, they make possible the study of social and religious history in the Greek and Roman contexts.

In the field of Christian Studies, epitaphs have drawn much less attention. This circumstance is attributable to several factors. There is first and foremost the scarcity of identifiably Christian epitaphs dating from the Roman imperial period (first-third centuries C.E.), as well as the general decline in the overall production of carved stone monuments thereafter in the Roman world. The surviving Christian funerary monuments with engraved epitaphs simply number several tens of thousands fewer than the non-Christian. In fact, pre-fourth century Christian funerary inscriptions occur in significant concentrations only in two places within the territory of the Roman Empire: in the catacombs of the city of Rome and in central Anatolia. Of these two concentrations, the latter provides inscriptions which are more diverse, more generally informative, and noteworthy for being carved on above-ground, publicly visible monuments. Thus the focus of this collection.

The study of Christian epitaphs also has been hampered by their erratic publication. For the most part, the epitaphs have been buried (so to speak) within the classical epigraphical corpora, or scattered through a plethora of

1

sometimes obscure books, journals, and bulletins, none of which are attuned primarily to Christian Studies. All of the epitaphs collected here have been published previously, and most of them have been published more than once. The intent has been to assemble a representative sample of the early-Christian epitaphs of Anatolia, to advertise their existence, and to illuminate their character and possibilities.

The collection has been divided into topical chapters, each with a separate introduction. This division is meant to highlight specific categories of problems and/or data offered by the epitaphs. Within each chapter, the major concern has been for simplicity and readability. Commentary on the Greek text has been minimized. Discussion of the many peculiarities of grammar, spelling, etc., which occur in epitaphs would have added significantly to the bulk of this volume. Notes pertaining to other matters likewise have been abbreviated.

However, a select publication history for each epitaph has been provided. The works cited in the publication histories have been limited to those most recent in date, most readily available, and/or which provide the most useful commentary. The publication histories serve as a bibliography and a guide to more detailed textual and/or topical commentary.

These epitaphs raise many questions about the life of Christians in Roman Anatolia, their relations with their non-Christian neighbors and with various levels of government, their attitudes towards life and death and religion, and so on. No attempt has been made here to expound on these questions.

CHAPTER 1

THE ANATOLIAN EPITAPH

Funerary monuments in Greco-Roman Anatolia during the Roman imperial period were constructed in a variety of forms. Those monuments which have survived, either in whole or in part, were constructed of stone — most commonly marble or limestone. The individual forms of stone monument included the free-standing sarcophagus; upright slab (stele), columnar, or altar-shaped (bomos) tombstone; crematory urn and/or statuary with pedestal. Two or more of these forms were sometimes combined as part of a more elaborate funerary complex or mausoleum. (no. 1.1)

Our knowledge is very scant concerning both the original setting of the surviving monuments and their precise relationship to the burial proper. Very few ancient funerary monuments in Anatolia have survived completely intact, and virtually none have survived undisturbed and still containing (or in proximity to) identifiable human remains. Not many graveyard sites from the period even are known. A large percentage of the surviving monuments have been plowed up randomly by modern farmers or found as reused stone in later structures: walls, foundations, etc. Many monuments (now lost) are known only from the drawings and notations of nineteenth and early-twentieth century travellers.

The funerary monuments normally were decorated with various sorts of ornamental carvings: portraits (both of humans and of divinities); representations of the funeral, or of daily life, or of such specific aspects of daily life as the occupational tools of the deceased; floral patterns; wreaths; stylized architectural details; etc. At the very least, the monument was equipped with an engraved inscription/epitaph. Because of their fragmentary condition, the presence of the epitaph often is the only feature which identifies the funerary character of surviving parts of the monuments.

The large majority of these epitaphs were written in Greek. Far less numerous were those written in Latin (no. 4.4) or in native Anatolian dialects (using Greek characters.) A rare few contained Hebrew, a language not understood (apparently) even by most Anatolian Jews. Throughout Anatolia, epitaphs tended to be rather formulaic and to express certain more-or-less standard motifs. This circumstance reflects the role of the professional stoneworker in framing most epitaphs.

3

A funerary monument usually was the joint creation of the purchaser/dedicant and of a professional stoneworker. The particular contributions of each party are difficult to delineate clearly in the finished product, but there can be little doubt that the stoneworker tended to be the most influential partner. Considerable evidence indicates that tombstones commonly were offered for sale already fully carved except for the epitaphs — a method of marketing common today, which allows the typical purchaser only a minimal influence on the design of the stone. Some ancient epitaphs, for example, overflowed the area prepared originally to contain them and had to be completed in haphazard fashion, squeezed between other, previously-wrought design elements. Furthermore, the repetitious, formulaic nature of the epitaphs likely stems (in part) from the use of catalogues of stock phrases, verses, and formulae, which were available in the stoneyards to prompt even the textual choices of customers.

Admittedly, the individual purchaser of a monument was able to influence the finished product (including the epitaph) in a purely personal way if desired. Some of the stones show clear signs of erasures and/or alterations of original design elements which do not appear to be corrections of mistakes. These modifications may have been ordered by purchasers who were not satisfied completely with the selection of ready-carved designs available to them; and, indeed, a few epitaphs do identify the purchaser/dedicant directly as the author of the epitaph and/or suggest that the dedicant had some role in conceiving and/or executing the total work. (nos. 2.15, 3.5, 4.11) Yet we must wonder how many purchasers would have been willing or able to pay for extra (or custom) stonework or likely to replicate independently widely-used, formulaic expressions.

The specific dominant formulae, funerary vocabulary, and ornamental decorations varied considerably (sometimes) even from city to city within Anatolia. To cite only one example, a number of different words were used to designate a sarcophagus, each one more widely used in some areas than in others: σωματοθήκη, πύελος, σορός, σκάφη, etc. Some of these variations may stem from genuine regional differences, but others may reflect only coincidental differences in the work-a-day repertoires of local stoneworkers.

The funerary monument in Roman Anatolia served approximately the same purposes as do modern funerary monuments. Primarily, the monument served to commemorate the deceased, whose name(s) was(were) preserved in the epitaph. The simplest of the epitaphs, in fact, consisted merely of a name. (no. 1.2) To this nucleus, miscellaneous facts usually were added in order to distinguish the individual life and personality behind the name. Epitaphs prepared posthumously by the family or friends of the deceased routinely cited such details as the person's age at death, place or circumstances of death, commendable personal traits, occupation, or honors. (nos. 1.3, 1.4) Those dedicating the monument also commonly augmented the epitaph with their own names and their relationship to the deceased. (nos. 1.5, 1.6) On the other hand, numerous individuals prepared their own monuments prior to their own death. This fact was explicitly related in many epitaphs. These epitaphs necessarily could not be informative about death, but still served to advertise the name and the personal circumstances and/or accomplishments of the deceased. (nos. 1.7, 1.8)

Greco-Roman society in Anatolia also was peculiarly anxious to preserve the strict exclusivity and inviolability of the tomb, especially the family tomb. This concern, which may have stemmed from Anatolian ideas about the circumstances of the dead, was voiced directly and with considerable regularity in the epitaphs. Quite a large number of Anatolian epitaphs commemorated multiple individuals from a single family, all or most of whom often still were living when the monument was dedicated. The epitaphs listed specifically all those individuals who were authorized to be buried in the tomb. Such epitaphs commonly included a blatant warning to potential violators of the tomb, particularly to those who might attempt to deposit an unauthorized corpse in the tomb. Typically, the potential violator was threatened with the imposition of a monetary fine of specified amount, to be paid to a specified authority — most often the city treasury or the imperial fiscus. (no. 1.9) Presumably, these authorities accepted responsibility in this regard, for some epitaphs even included the information that a copy of the epitaph was on file in the city archives. (no. 1.11) Alternatively (and especially in central Anatolia), potential violators of the tomb also were threatened with divine retribution and placed under a curse. The threat of supernatural intervention was used both in place of and coupled together with the threat of a fine. (nos. 1.1, 1.10, 1.11, 1.16, 1.17, 1.18, 1.20, 1.22, 1.23, 1.24 *et al.*)

In some areas of Anatolia, epitaphs customarily included the date of dedication. A number of dated epitaphs originated in cities of western and/or central Anatolia, which had been a part of the original Roman province of Asia. These cities usually reckoned dates by numbering the years of a provincial era which had begun with the reconstitution of Asia accomplished by C. Cornelius Sulla in 85 B.C.E. (nos. 1.19, 1.23) In other Anatolian locales, different provincial eras were in use, and a few Anatolian epitaphs were dated by reference to the serving Roman proconsular governor. (no. 1.11)

Even epitaphs which were not explicitly dated sometimes contain information which is useful for estimating the general date of a monument. In fact, the very names of the deceased/dedicants can sometimes be helpful. The most important example concerns the name Aurelios/Aurelia. This name was widely adopted as a badge of Roman citizenship after the emperor Caracalla (named officially, M. Aurelius Antoninus) granted the Roman citizenship to all

5

free inhabitants of the Roman Empire in C.E. 212. In Anatolia, the use of the name Aurelios/Aurelia generally indicates a date after 212 and probably not much later than 400. (nos. 1.9, 1.10, 1.11, 1.14, 1.16, 1.19, 1.22, 1.23, 1.24 *et al.*)

Remarkably few epitaphs contained direct statements of religious affiliation. (1.12) Most did not allude even to religion. The overwhelming majority of the population of Anatolia probably continued to adhere to classical, Greco-Roman/native Anatolian polytheism at least down into the fourth century; but clear expression of this majority religious preference normally appeared in the epitaphs only in an indirect and/or incidental way. For example, the dedication θεοῖς καταχθονίοις, "To the katachthonic gods (i.e. gods of the dead)," became somewhat common in Anatolian epitaphs, perhaps in imitation of the customary western/Latin dedication, *Dis Manibus.* (no. 1.13; see also no. 1.14 — a different example of religious notation). However, explicit information concerning religious preference appeared most often in the context of the warning against violation of the tomb. Temples sometimes were the specified receivers of fine payments (nos. 1.15, 1.16), and curse formulae sometimes were fairly specific in identifying the avenging deity. (nos. 1.16, 1.17, 1.18)[1]

Anatolia's considerable Jewish population requires little separate attention in the present context. For the most part, Jewish funerary monuments were indistinguishable from the non-Jewish majority in artistic style, in nomenclature, and in the formulation of the epitaph.[2] The fact of the deceased and/or dedicant being a Jew was hardly ever addressed directly. (no. 1.19) A few monuments were decorated with such exclusively Jewish symbols as the menorah, and very rarely with Hebrew characters; but most of the surviving Jewish monuments are recognizable as such only because the Jews of Anatolia were as concerned as everybody else in their environment to protect the inviolability of the tomb. The synagogue like the traditional temples was sometimes designated to receive fines paid for violation of the tomb. (nos. 1.20, 1.21) Certain curse formulae also seem likely to point to Jewish authorship, but (as discussed in Chapter 2) potential confusion of Jewish and Christian epitaphs is a persistent problem. (nos. 1.20, 1.22, 1.23, 1.24)

---

[1] For more information see J.H.M. Strubbe, "Cursed be he that moves my bones," in C.A. Faraone and D. Obbink, eds., *Magika Hiera: Ancient Greek Magic and Religion* (Oxford: Oxford University Press, 1991) 33–59.

[2] See Pieter W. van der Horst, *Ancient Jewish Epitaphs* (Kampen, The Netherlands: Kok Pharos Publishing House, 1991).

(1.1) Limestone stele from Choghu/Appola.

"Ος ἂν κακῶς ποιήσει / ταῖς σοροῖς ἢ τῷ /
τάφῳ ἢ τῷ στεγνῷ / ἢ τοῖς δένδρασιν ὁ /
θεὸς αὐτῷ προσκόψαι–/ το ὁράσει τέκνοις βί–/
4   ῳ καὶ προίδοιτο τέ–/ κνα λίποιτο χῆρον /
βίον οἶκον ἔρημον.

1. σοροῖς (σορός) = sarcophagus was used throughout Anatolia, but was especially prominent at Hierapolis in Phrygia and Aphrodisias in Caria. See Jadwiga Kubinska, *Les Monuments funéraires dans les Inscriptions grecques de l'Asie mineure* (Warsaw: Center for Mediterranean Archeology, Polish Academy of Sciences, 1968) 32.

4. The translation of προίδοιτο τέκνα is suggested by W.M. Calder, "Julia-Ipsus and Augustopolis," *JRS* 2 (1912) 254.

(1.2) Stele (?) from the territory of Iznik/Nikaea.

Ἀριστόνικος
Παυσανίου.

(1.1) Limestone stele from Choghu/Appola.[3]

> Whoever should do damage either to the sarcophagi or
> to the tomb or to the shelter or to the trees, may
> the god[4] strike against his eyesight, his children and his
> livelihood; and may he see his children
> dead before him, and leave behind bereaved
> life and a deserted house.[5]

Publication: *MAMA* 1, no. 437; W.M. Calder, "Julia-Ipsus and Augustopolis," *JRS* 2 (1912) 254, no. 12.

(1.2) Stele (?) from the territory of Iznik/Nikaea.

> Aristonikos
> son of Pausanios.

Publication: Şahin, *Iznik* 2.1, no. 763; G. Mendel, "Inscriptions de Bithynie," *BCH* 24 (1900) 384, no. 36.

---

[3] This stele obviously is no more than a warning sign set up to protect a tomb complex which encompassed a grove of trees, some sort of permanent building and multiple sarcophagi. Nothing but the stele has survived.

[4] The god probably is Zeus Alsenos, god of the grove, who is referred to explicitly in *MAMA* 1, nos. 435, 435a. See the commentary on this inscription in W.M. Calder, "Julia-Ipsus and Augustopolis," *JRS* 2 (1912) 254.

[5] Cf. the curses in nos. 1.10, 2.8, and see Louis Robert, "Malédictions funéraires grecques," *CRAI* (1978) 255ff.

(1.3) Stele from Izmit/Nikomedia.

> Δεῖος Δείου
> ζήσας ἔτη κη'
> τελευτήσας
> 4 ἐν Ποτιώ–
> λοις. χαῖ–
> ρε.

1. Δεῖος = Δῖος. Confusion of ι and ει is very common in the Anatolian epitaphs. Note throughout the collection examples of ἰ = εἰ, ἰς = εἰς, and ind. a. 3 sg. verb endings in ι, etc. See also nos. 2.1, 2.2, 2.3 *et al.*: Χρειστιανοί.

(1.4) Marble stele from Iznik/Nikaea.

> Κλαύδιος Θάλλος
> Γ(άιου) Κλαυδίου
> Καλπορνια–
> 4 νοῦ οἰκονόμ–
> ος ζήσας ἔτη ν'.

(1.3) Stele from Izmit/Nikomedia.

> Deios son of Deios,
> who lived to age 28
> and who died
> in Puteolis.
> Farewell.

Publication: *TAM* 4.1, no. 125; *IGR* 3, no. 13; *CIG*, no. 3780.

(1.4) Marble stele from Iznik/Nikaea.

> Klaudios Thallos,
> steward[6] of Gaios
> Klaudios Kalpornianos,
> you lived to age 50.

Publication: Şahin, *Iznik* 1, no. 205.

---

[6] Concerning the position of οἰκονόμος/steward see Louis Robert, *Etudes anatoliennes* (Paris: E. de Boccard, 1937; reprinted Amsterdam: A.M. Hakkert, 1970) 241–42.

(1.5) Sarcophagus from Izmit/Nikomedia.

Αἰμιλίαι Παύληι Αἰμιλίου
Παύλου θυγατρὶ Αἰλί<α> Ἀσκλη–
πιοδότη ἡ μήτηρ τὴν πύαι–
4 λον ἐκ τῶν ἰδίων, ζησάσῃ
ἔτη ιβ'. χαίρετε.

1. Αἰμιλίαι Παύληι. Iota postscripts often are not carved on the stones. Many epigraphical publications purposely do not add iota subscripts to edited texts unless the iota actually is present, but subscripts have been added where appropriate in this collection.

3–4. πύαιλον = πύελον. Confusion of αι and ε also is very common in the epitaphs. Note throughout κέ = καί, ἔστε = ἔσται, χέρετε = χαίρετε, etc. Originally meaning "feeding-trough" or "bathtub," πύελος was the typical designation of "sarcophagus" in the region of Nikomedia. See Kubinska, *Les Monuments*, 48ff.

(1.5) Sarcophagus from Izmit/Nikomedia.

> For Aimilia Paula, daughter
> of Aimilios Paulos,[7] Ailia
> Asklepiodote, her mother,
> (acquired) this sarcophagus, out of her own
> funds.
> She lived to age 12. Farewell.

Publication: *TAM* 4.1, no. 235.

---

[7] The father of the girl presumably was dead already.

(1.6) Marble plaque from Iznik/Nikaea ? (in the Louvre).

Τὸν θρασὺν ἐν σταδίοις ἐσο–
[ρᾷ]ς με νέκυν, παροδεῖτα, Ταρ–
[σέ]α ῥητιάριν, δεύτερον πάλον,
4 [Μ]ελάνιππον. οὐκέτι χαλκε[λ]-
άτου φωνὴν σάλπιγγος ἀκο[ύω]
[οὐ]δ᾽ ἀνίσων αὐλῶν κέλαδον ἀ–
[εθ]λῶν ἀνεγείρω· φασὶν δ᾽ Ἡρα[κ]-
8 [λ]έα δυοκαίδεκα ἆθλα τελέσσ[αι]·
[τα]ὐτὰ δ᾽ ἐγὼ τελέσας τρισκαίδεκα τ[ὸ]
τέλος ἔσχον.

Θάλλος καὶ Ζόη Μελανίππ[ῳ]
12 μνείας χάριν ἐκ τῶν ἰδίων
ἐποίησαν.

3. δεύτερον πάλον was apparently a rank of gladiators. See Louis Robert, *Les Gladiateurs dans l'Orient grec* (Paris: de Boccard, 1940; reprinted Amsterdam: Hakkert, 1971) 28ff.

6. αὐλῶν. M.L. West, *Ancient Greek Music* (Oxford: Clarendon, 1992) energetically attacks the conventional translation of αὐλός as "flute." See pp. 1 and 81–85. Because the instrument appears to have had a double-reed mouthpiece, West prefers to call it an "oboe."

(1.6) Marble plaque from Iznik/Nikaea ? (in the Louvre).

> A courageous man in the amphitheatre, look
> at me (now), a corpse, O passerby — the
> Tarsan retiarius[8] of the second lot,
> Melanippos. No more the
> sound of the brass trumpet do I hear,
> nor do I rouse the clamour of the multi-tone
> pipes of the arena. They say that
> Herakles performed twelve labors;
> in the same way, I, having accomplished thirteen,
> reached the end.

> Thallos and Zoe, for Melanippos,
> in memory, out of their own funds
> commissioned (this).

Publication: Şahin, *Iznik* 1, no. 277; Louis Robert, *Les Gladiateurs dans l'Orient grec* (Paris: E. de Boccard, 1940; reprinted Amsterdam: Hakkert, 1971) 234, no. 298; *IGR* 3, no. 43; *CIG*, no. 3765.

---

[8] The retiarius was a type of lightly-armed gladiator, whose special weapon was a net.

(1.7) Pedestal from Izmit/Nikomedia.

> Μ(άρκος) ᾿Ιούλιο[ς]
> Θεόδοτο[ς]
> στρατευσάμενο[ς]
> 4 ἐπιτείμα[ς]
> τὸν ἀνδριάντ[α]
> ζῶν ἑαυτῷ
> [κ]ατεσκεύασα.
> 8 χαῖρε.

(1.8) Limestone stele from Serai önü/Laodikea Katakekaumene.

> Θάλαμος
> καὶ Χρησ–
> τὴ κυρίων
> 4 Καισάρων
> δοῦλοι ἐ–
> αυτοῖς
> ζῶντες
> 8 μνήμη[ς]
> ἕνεκεν.

(1.7) Pedestal from Izmit/Nikomedia.

> Markos Ioulios
> Theodotos,
> who served as a soldier
> with honor,
> while still living,
> constructed this statue
> for himself.
> Farewell.

Publication: *TAM* 4.1, no. 203; *IGR* 3, no.9.

(1.8) Limestone stele from Serai önü/Laodikea Katakekaumene.

> Thalamos
> and Chreste,
> slaves of the lords
> Caesars,
> (acquired this)
> for themselves
> while still living
> as a memorial.

Publication: *MAMA* 1, no.29; W.M. Ramsay (ed.), *Studies in the History and Art of the Eastern Provinces of the Roman Empire* (Aberdeen University Studies 20; Aberdeen: Aberdeen University Press, 1906) 67, no. 35.

(1.9) Sarcophagus lid from Ladik/Laodikea Katakekaumene.

Αὐρ(ήλιος) Μ[εν]έδημος Ἀντωνεί–
νου Αὐρ(ηλίᾳ) Τάτει συμβίῳ γλυ–
κυτάτῃ κὲ Μενεδήμῳ υἱ–
4 ᾧ αὐτῶν μνήμης χάριν·
ὃς δὲ μετὰ ἡμᾶς ἕτερον
τινα ἐπενβάλῃ, δώσει
τῷ φίσκῳ ✳ ,α.

5–6. ὃς...ἐπενβάλῃ. This formulaic expression with ἐπεμβάλλω (referring to the insertion of an unauthorized body into the tomb) appears often in epitaphs from the region of Laodikea Katakekaumene. The substitution of ν for μ before β is typical. Cf. no. 3.11 and note no. 3.7, where ἐπιβάλλω is used with the same sense.

7. ✳ = a standard abbreviation for "denarii."

(1.10) Stele from Kadin Khan/Laodikea Katakekaumene.

Σεξτίλιος καὶ / Ἀντέστιος Αὐρ(ηλίου) /
Γλύκωνος πατρὶ / ἑαυτῶν καὶ μη–/
τρὶ αὐτῶν μνήμης / χάριν· /
4 ὃς δὲ ταύτῃ [τῇ] / σ[ή]λῃ χεῖρα κακή[ν] /
προσοί<σ>ει ὀρφανὰ τέ[κνα] /
λίποιτο κῆρον βίο[ν] /
οἶκον ἔρημον.

4. χεῖρα κακή[ν]. The laying on of "evil (or evil-doing) hands" was a common description of violation/abuse. Cf. no. 2.16.

6. κῆρον = χῆρον.

18

(1.9) Sarcophagus lid from Ladik/Laodikea Katakekaumene.

> Aurelios Menedemos, son of Antoneinos,
> (erected this) for (his) dearest wife, Aurelia
> Tateis, and their son, Menedemos,
> in memory.
> Whoever should insert another
> after us, will pay
> 1000 denarii to the fiscus.

Publication: *MAMA* 7, no. 29b.

(1.10) Stele from Kadin Khan/Laodikea Katakekaumene.

> Sextilios and Antestios, sons of Aurelios
> Glykon, (erected this) for their father and mother,
> in memory. Whoever should lay evil hands
> on this stele will leave behind orphaned children,
> bereaved life, and a deserted house.[9]

Publication: *MAMA* 7, no. 28.

---

[9] Cf. the curses of nos. 1.1 and 2.8, and note Gibson, *CFC*, 37, no. 16, in which the last two elements are transposed: i.e., ... οἶκον χῆρον βίον ἔρημον. The transposition could reflect carelessness on the part of the letter carver in applying an often-used formula.

(1.11) Bomos (?) from Seulun/Dokimeion.

Αὐρήλιος Εἰρηναῖος ᾿Αριστω–
νύμου ἐπεσκεύασεν τὸ προ–
γο[νικὸν] μνημεῖον ζῶν ἑαυ–
4 τῷ [καὶ γ]ονεῦσι καὶ Αὐρηλίᾳ
᾿Α[μιᾳ τ]ῇ ἑαυτοῦ γυναικὶ
[καὶ τέκ]νοις Αὐρηλίῳ Παν–
μ[ένει] καὶ Αὐρηλίῳ ᾿Αμια–
8 νῷ· τίς ἂν δὲ τούτῳ τῷ
μνημείῳ κακὸν προσπ[οι]ή–
σει ἢ ἕτερον πτῶμα [ἐπισκομί–]
σει ἢ τῆς δο[ύλης] μου Κοσμίας]
12 ἀποτεί[σει τῷ ἱερωτάτῳ τα–]
μείῳ δη[νάρια δισχίλια πεντα–]
κόσια [καὶ αὐτὸς ἔστω τέκνων]
[τέκνοις ὑποκα]τάρα[τος· {τούτου}]
16 [τούτου τὸ ἀτίγραφον ἀπετέθη εἰς τὰ]
ἀρχεῖα ᾿Ανεικίῳ Φ[αύστ]ῳ ἀνθυπά[τ]ῳ.

3. μνημεῖον was one of the most widely-used terms for "tomb" (and sometimes "sarcophagus") in Anatolian epitaphs. See Kubinska, *Les Monuments*, 15ff.

8. τίς = ὅστις. This substitution appears frequently in the epitaphs.

12–13. ἱερωτάτῳ ταμείῳ = imperial fiscus. See Louis Robert, *Villes d'Asie mineure* (2d ed.; Paris: E. de Boccard, 1962) 283; Hugh J. Mason, *Greek Terms for Roman Institutions* (American Studies in Papyrology 13; Toronto: A.M. Hakkert, 1974) 91, 187.

(1.11) Bomos (?) from Seulun/Dokimeion.[10]

> Aurelios Eirenaios, son of Aristonymos,
> while still living, restored the ancestral
> tomb for himself and for his parents,
> and for Aurelia Amia, his wife, and
> for his children: Aurelios Panmeneos
> amd Aurelios Amianos. Whoever should
> do damage to this tomb or install
> an additional corpse, other than that of my
> slave Kosmia, will pay to the
> imperial fiscus 2500 denarii and
> be cursed to his children's children.[11]
> A copy of this [epitaph] has been
> stored in the archives. Aneikios
> Phaustos proconsul.[12]

Publication: *MAMA* 4, no. 27; *CIG*, no. 3882; W.J. Hamilton, *Researches in Asia Minor, Pontus and Armenia* (2 vols.; London, 1842) 2, no. 175.

---

[10] The restorations of the Greek text (except in line 17) are based upon the copy of W.J. Hamilton, *Researches in Asia Minor, Pontus, and Armenia* (2 vols; London, 1842) 2, no. 175.

[11] The continuation of the curse unto the "children's children" has been said to "recall the language of the Old Testament," and thus to indicate Jewish authorship. This is far from certain, however. See A. R. R. Sheppard, "Jews, Christians, and Heretics in Acmonia and Eumeneia," *AS* 29 (1979) 175.

[12] Q. Anicius Faustus was proconsul C.E. 217/218.

(1.12) Marble stele from Sultandere/Dorylaeum.

> Χρυσόγονος κὲ Εὐτ-
> υχίων κὲ ᾽Ελεύθερος
> κὲ ᾽Αφροδεισία πατρὶ
> 4 ᾽Επαφροδείτῳ κὲ μητρὶ
> ῾Ηδονῇ γλυκυτάτοις
> μνήμης χάρ[ι]ν κὲ Διὶ Βρον-
> τῶντι εὐχήν.

(1.13) Marble pedestal with crematory urn from Izmit/Nikomedia.

> θεοῖς
> Μᾶρκος ἐριοπώλης Σωστράτη τε σύμβιος
> ζῶντες ἑαυτοῖς τὴν ὀστοθήκην. χαίρετε.
> 4 καταχθονίοις

3. ὀστοθήκη(ν) = "urn" appears densely in Bithynia, Galatia, Ionia, and Lycia; and sporadically elsewhere. In Bithynia, the urn typically was placed atop a funerary altar/bomos. See Kubinska, *Les Monuments*, 64ff.

(1.12) Marble stele from Sultandere/Dorylaeum.

> Chrysogonos and Eutychion
> and Eleutheros
> and Aphrodeisia (erected this)
> for (their) dearest father, Epaphrodeitos,
> and (their) dearest mother, Hedone,
> in memory, and as a votive to
> Zeus Bronton.[13]

Publication: *MAMA* 5, no. 111.

(1.13) Marble pedestal with crematory urn from Izmit/Nikomedia.

> To the katachthonic gods:
> Markos, a wool dealer, and Sostrate, (his) wife,
> while still living, (acquired) for themselves
> this urn (and pedestal). Farewell.

Publication: *TAM* 4.1, no. 174; F.K. Dörner, "Inschriften und Denkmäler aus Bithynien," *Istanbuler Forschungen* 14 (1941) 88, no. 87.

---

[13] For Zeus Bronton see *MAMA* 5, pp. xxxviii–xliv.

(1.14) Sarcophagus from Hierapolis.

Ἡ σορὸς καὶ ὁ βωμὸς Ἰουλίου Μακεδονικοῦ, ἐν ᾗ /
κηδευθῇ ὁ Μακεδονικὸς καὶ ἡ σύμβιος αὐτοῦ
Α(ὐ)ρ(ηλία / Ἰουλία, καὶ μηδ[ενὶ] ἑτέρῳ ἔξον
4 κηδευθῆναι· ἂν οὐ ἀπο–/ τείσει τῷ φίσκῳ ✶ φ'·
[ἔδ]οσαν δὲ οἱ Μακεδονικο[ῦ] τοῖς σημια–/
φόροι<ς> τοῦ Ἀρχηγέτου Ἀπόλλωνος στεφανωτικὸν
μη(νὸς) / ι' ✶ ζσθ' / καὶ [μη(νὸς)] α', γ' ✶ ζσθ'.

(1.15) Sarcophagus from Termessos.

[Χ]ρυσόγονος καὶ Σευηρι–
[α]νός, οἱ Ἑρμ[ο]ῦ Πάπου,
τὴν σωματοθήκην
4 Ἑρμῇ, τῷ πατρί, καὶ
Ηδονῇ, τῇ συμβί–
ῳ τοῦ Ἑρμοῦ, καὶ τ–
οῖς ἐκ τοῦ Ἑρμοῦ·
8 μηδενὶ δὲ ἄλλῳ
ἐξεῖνε, ἐπεὶ ὁ
πειράσας ἐκτείσει Διὶ Σολυ–
μεῖ ✶ ,β.

3. σωματοθήκη(ν) was the primary term for "sarcophagus" used at
Termessos. See Kubinska, *Les Monuments*, 32ff. and no. 1.16 below.

(1.14) Sarcophagus from Hierapolis.

> The sarcophagus and the bomos (are those) of Ioulios
> Makedonikos, in which have been interred Makedonikos
> and his wife, Aurelia (?) Ioulia, and for no other
> is it possible to be interred (here). (Whoever)
> should not (observe this stipulation), will pay
> to the fiscus 500 denarii. The family of
> Makedonikos bequeathed to the Semiaphoroi of
> Apollon Archegetos[14] 7209 denarii for the laying
> of garlands (on the tomb) on month 10 (day?) and
> 7209 denarii for the laying of garlands on month 1, day 3.

Publication: Ramsay, *CB* 1, 115, no. 19.

(1.15) Sarcophagus from Termessos.

> Chrysogonos and Seuerianos, sons of Hermes Papos,
> (acquired this) sarcophagus for Hermes, (their) father,
> and for Hedone, wife of Hermes, and
> for those descended from Hermes.
> For no other is (burial here) allowed.
> For that, the perpetrator will pay to (the temple of) Zeus
> Solymos 2000 denarii.

Publication: *TAM* 3.1, no. 812.

---

[14] Concerning the Semiaphoroi, see the discussion in W.M. Ramsay, *The Cities and Bishoprics of Phrygia*, (2 vols.; Oxford: Clarendon, 1895–96) 1:96ff.

(1.16) Sarcophagus from Termessos.

> Αὐρ(ήλιος) Χρυσόγονος Ἑρμαίου τὴν
> σωματοθήκην ἑαυτῷ καὶ Αὐρ(ηλία)
> Πρωτογενία / τῇ γυν[αικὶ αὐ]τοῦ
> 4 καὶ Αὐρ(ηλία) Ἀρτεμει, τῇ
> προενούσῃ αὐτοῦ
> ἀδελφῇ· ἑτέρῳ δὲ μὴ
> ἐξὸν εἶναι ἐπιθάψαι
> 8 τινά ἐπεὶ ὁ πειράσας
> ἐκτείσι Διὶ Σολυμεῖ ✳,β
> καὶ ἔσται αὐτῷ κα< ὶ> πρὸς
> τοὺς κατοιχομένους.

(1.17) Stele from Iznik/Nikaea.

> [- - - - - - - - -]
> ὃς ἂν δὲ εἰς τοῦτο
> τὸ μνημεῖον δόλον
> πονηρὸν πυήσει, πα–
> 4 [ρ]αδίδωμι αὐτὸν θεο[ῖ]–
> [ς] καταχθονίοις.
> ἀνεξοδίαστον.

6. ἀνεξοδίαστον (an expression referring to the inalienability of the tomb) appears densely in epitaphs in the region of Nikaea and almost nowhere else. See Louis Robert, *Hellenica* 1 (Paris: Maisonneuve, 1940) 60ff.; *Hellenica* 2 (Paris: Maisonneuve, 1946) 147–48.

26

(1.16) Sarcophagus from Termessos.

> Aurelios Chrysogonos, son of Hermaios,
> (acquired this) sarcophagus for himself
> and for his wife Aurelia Protogenia,
> and for Aurelia Artemis, his sister —
> already interred. For no other is it
> allowable to bury someone (here).
> For that, the perpetrator will pay
> to Zeus Solymos 2000 denarii, and
> also he will reckon with the dead.[15]

Publication: *TAM* 3.1, no. 813.

(1.17) Stele from Iznik/Nikaea.

> ... whoever should do evil treachery
> to this monument/tomb, I will
> consign to the katachthonic gods.
> Inalienable.

Publication: Şahin, *Iznik*, 1, no 87; G. Mendel, "Inscriptions de Bithynie," *BCH* 24 (1900) 392, no. 54.

---

[15] Cf. the curses in nos. 1.23, 1.24 and the Christian (Eumeneian Formula) curse which appears numerous times in the chapters following.

(1.18) Stele from Akşehir/Philomelion.

Τίς ἂν ὧδε
ὁρκίσει εἶ-
ναι πρὸς
4 Διὸς κατ[ά]-
ρη

(1.19) Stele (?) from Aghar-Hissar/Diokleia.

Ἔτους τμβ'
Αὐ[ρ(ήλιος)] ᾽Αλέξανδ[ρος]
᾽Ιουδαῖος [ζῶν] κατεσκεύ[ασε]
4 τὸ μνη[μῖον].

(1.18) Stele from Akşehir/Philomelion.

> (Upon) whoever should
> swear an oath here (by the body of the
> dead ?), there will be a curse
> from Zeus.

Publication: *MAMA* 7, no. 192.

(1.19) Stele (?) from Aghar-Hissar/Diokleia.

> (In the) year 342 (Sullan Era = C.E. 257)
> Aurelios Alexandros, a Jew,
> while still living, constructed
> this memorial/tomb.

Publication: J.B. Frey, *Corpus Inscriptionum Iudaicarum* (2 vols.; Rome: Pontificio Istituto di Archeologia Cristiana, 1952) 2, no. 764; Ramsay, *CB* 2, no. 562.

(1.20) Marble bomos from Izmit/Nikomedia.

[- - - - - - - - - -]
τὴν θήκην ἔθηκα
καὶ τὸν βωμὸν
τῇ γλυκυτάτῃ τεκού–
4 σῃ Οὐλπίᾳ Καπιτύλλῃ·
καὶ βούλομε ἕτερον
μηδέν<α> ἀνασκεβάσ[ε]·
εἰ μή, ἕξει πρὸς τ[ὴν]
8 κρίσιν καὶ δώσε[ι]
τῇ συναγωγῇ ✳ ,α
καὶ τῷ ταμείῳ
✳ φ'.
12 χαίρετε.

1. θήκη(ν) = sarcophagus was especially common in Cilicia and at Termessos. See Kubinska, *Les Monuments*, 38ff.

3–4. τεκούσῃ = mother. See Louis Robert, *Hellenica* 11–12 (Paris: Maisonneuve, 1960) 388–89.

6. ἀνασκεβάσ[ε] = ἀνασκευάσαι.

(1.20) Marble bomos from Izmit/Nikomedia.

>[I, _____,]... prepared this sarcophagus
>and bomos
>for my dearest mother,
>Oulpia Kapitylla,
>and I want no other
>to dismantle it.
>Otherwise, he will answer
>to the judgment (of God)[16] and
>pay 1000 denarii to the synagogue,
>and 500 denarii to the (city?) treasury.
>Farewell.

Publication: *TAM* 4.1, no. 376; Louis Robert, *Hellenica* 11–12 (Paris: Maisonneuve, 1960) 387ff.

---

[16] Cf. the curse in no. 1.22 and see note 15 above.

(1.21) Stele (?) from Izmit/Nikomedia.

[- - - - - - - - - -]
[μηδένα ἕτερον κατατ]εθῆν[αι· ἐὰν]
[δέ τι]ς τολμήσῃ, δ[ώ]–
σει προστείμ[ου]
4   τῇ συναγωγῇ τῶν
     Ἰυδέων ✱,α καὶ
     τῷ ταμίῳ ✱,β. χαίρετε.

(1.22) Stele from Izmit/Nikomedia.

Αὐρ(ήλιος) Κυρίων / ζῶν ἐμαυτῷ /
κατεσκεύασα / τὸ μνημῖον /
καὶ τῇ συνβίῳ / μου Αὐρ(ηλίᾳ) Ἰουλιάδι· /
4   καὶ βούλομαι με–/ τὰ τὸ ἐμὲ τεθῆ–/
     ναι μηδένα ἕτε–/ ρον τεθῆναι εἰ /
     μὴ τέκνον μου· / ὃς δὲ ἂν παρὰ /
     ταῦτά τι ποιή–/ σει, ἕξῃ κρίσιν /
8   πρὸς τὸν Θεόν. / Εὐλογία πᾶσ[ιν].

3. συνβίῳ = συμβίῳ appears often in the epitaphs. Cf. no. 1.9:
ἐπενβάλη = ἐπεμβάλη.

7–8. ἕξῃ κρίσιν πρὸς τὸν Θεόν = ἕξῃ κριτὴν πρὸς τὸν Θεόν(?). Cf.
Ramsay, CB 2, 537, no. 394: ἔστε αὐτῷ πρὸς τὸν κριτὴν Θεόν.

(1.21) Stele (?) from Izmit/Nikomedia.

[. . . and I want no other to be put here.]

[In case anyone] should dare (to inter another),

he will pay 1000 denarii as a fine

to the synagogue of the Jews,

and 2000 denarii to the (city?) treasury. Farewell.

Publication: *TAM* 4.1, no. 377; Louis Robert, *Hellenica* 11–12 (Paris: Maisonneuve, 1960) 391 ff; J.B. Frey, *Corpus Inscriptionum Iudaicarum* (2 vols.; Rome: Pontificio Istituto Archeologia Cristiana, 1952) 2, no. 799.

(1.22) Stele from Izmit/Nikomedia.

I, Aurelios Kyrion, while still living constructed this

memorial for myself and for my wife, Aurelia Ioulias;

and after I am interred, I want no other to be put here

except my child. Whoever should do otherwise,

will answer to judgment before God. Blessing to all.[17]

Publication: *TAM* 4.1, no. 375; Louis Robert, *Hellenica* 11–12 (Paris: Maisonneuve, 1960) 392ff.

---

[17] The formula εὐλογία πᾶσιν seems commonly to be a Jewish formula and was often carved over the entry door to the synagogue. See Louis Robert, *Hellenica* 11–12 (Paris: Maisonneuve, 1960) 394, notes 4 and 5. This formula may establish (arguably) the Jewish origin of this monument and the Jewish character of the preceding curse, but van der Horst (*Ancient Jewish Epitaphs*, 18ff.) argues for the necessity of more rigorous (i.e., multiple) criteria.

(1.23) Bomos from Uşak/Akmonia (?).

(A) Ἔτους τλγ' / Αὐρ(ήλιος) Φρουγιανὸς /
Μηνοκρίτου καὶ Αὐρ(ηλία) /
Ἰουλιανὴ γυνὴ αὐτοῦ /
4 Μακαρίᾳ μητρὶ καὶ Ἀ–/ λεξανδρί–/
ᾳ θυγατρὶ /
γλυκυτάτῃ ζῶν–/ τες κατεσσκεύ–/
ασαν μνήμης / χάριν· /
8 εἰ δέ τις μετὰ τὸ τεθῆναι /
αὐτοὺς εἴ τις θάψει ἕτερον /
νεκρὸν ἢ ἀδικήσει λόγῳ /
ἀγορασίας, ἔσται αὐτῷ αἱ ἀραὶ /
12 ἢ γεγραμμέναι ἐν τῷ Δευτερο–/
νομίῳ

(B) ἀγορανομίᾳ
σειτωνείᾳ
16 παραφυλακείᾳ
πάσας ἀρχὰς
καὶ λειτουργί–
ας τελέσας καὶ
20 στρατηγήσαν–
τα.

11. ἀγορασίας. van der Horst, *Ancient Jewish Epitaphs*, 56, translates the word/phrase: "or commits injustice by buying (the place)."

(1.23) Bomos from Uşak/Akmonia (?).

> (A) (In the) year 333 (Sullan Era = C.E. 248)
> Aurelios Phrougianos, son of Menokritos, and
> Aurelia Iouliane, his wife, while still living,
> constructed (this) for Makaria,
> (his/her) mother, and for Alexandria,
> (their) dearest daughter, in memory.
> If, after they are interred, anyone should bury
> another corpse (here), or deliberately
> should abuse (this monument) by idling about (?)
> for him will be the curses which have been written
> in Deuteronomy.[18]

> (B) All duties and services
> being fulfilled for the
> offices of *agoranomos*,
> *seitonomos*, and *paraphylax*,
> (he) served also as
> *strategos*.[19]

Publication: *MAMA* 6, no. 335a; J.B. Frey, *Corpus Inscriptionum Iudaicarum* (2 vols.; Rome: Pontificio Istituto Archeologia Cristiana, 1952) 2, no. 760.

---

[18] The reference to "Deuteronomy" has been generally considered to prove the Jewish origin of the monument, especially since Akmonia provides other proof of a substantial Jewish population. Clearly, however, the reference is not unambiguous.

[19] Presumably, these civic offices were held by Aurelios Phrougianos, the dedicant. The *agoranomos* was the supervisor of the public market. The *seitonomos* supervised the grain supply. The *paraphylax* commanded a sort of rural police force, charged with keeping order in the city's outlying territory. The *strategos* was the chief magistrate. This man's career may illustrate the prominent role played by Jews in many cities of Anatolia.

(1.24) Marble bomos from Ishikli/Eumeneia.

[- - - - - - - - - -]
τὸν ἐπ' αὐτοῦ βωμὸν
κατεσκεύασεν Αὐρ(ήλιος)
Ζωτικὸς β' τοῦ Παπ[ι–(?)]
4 ου Εὐμενεὺς ἑαυτῷ
καὶ τῇ γυναικὶ αὐτοῦ
Αὐρηλίᾳ Ἀπφίῳ καὶ τῷ
ἀδελφῷ αὐτοῦ Ἀ–
8 [μ]μια[ν]ῷ κα[ὶ εἰ] τιν[ὶ]
[ἀλλ]ῷ α[ὐτ]ὸς ζῶν [συγ–]
[χω]ρήσει· οὐδενὶ δ[ὲ]
[ἀ]λλῷ ἐξὸν ἔσται
12 θεῖναι τινὰ· εἰ δέ τις
ἐπιχειρήσει, εἰσοίσει
ἰς τὴν Εὐμενέων βου–
λὴν προστείμου ✳ αφ'
16 καὶ ἔσται αὐτῷ πρὸς τὸ
μέγα ὄνομα τοῦ Θεοῦ.

(1.24) Marble bomos from Ishikli/Eumeneia.

> . . . Aurelios Zotikos the younger, son
> of Papias (?), a citizen of Eumeneia,
> constructed [the tomb] and the bomos
> nearby it for himself and for
> his wife, Aurelia Apphion, and for
> his brother Ammianos, and for any
> other he should agree to while still
> living. For no other person will it
> be possible to bury someone (here).
> If anyone should try, he will pay
> 1500 denarii to the *boule* of Eumeneia
> as a fine and he will reckon
> with the great Name of God.[20]

Publication: Sheppard, "Jews, Christians, and Heretics," 172–73; Ramsay, *CB* 2, 525, no. 369; *CIG*, no. 3902.

---

[20] Ramsay, *CB* 2, 525 classifies this monument as Christian, and the curse formula is one widely used by Christians. See discussion and examples of the Eumeneian Formula in the chapters following. Because of the reference to the "Name of God," however, the epitaph usually is classified as Jewish and the "Name" assumed to be the Tetragrammaton (YHWH). See, for example, Sheppard, "Jews, Christians, and Heretics," 173.

CHAPTER 2

THE CHRISTIAN EPITAPH

The funerary monuments/epitaphs of Christians in Roman imperial Anatolia differed little from those of non-Christians. The artistic style and selected motifs of the stonework, the phrasing and content of the epitaphs, and the apparent motivation behind the commissioning of the Christian monuments usually were very much in accord with normal Anatolian practices. The recognizably Christian character of these monuments does not seriously diminish their culturally homogenous appearance. In fact, the Christian character of a number of monuments only is evident precisely because the monuments **do** conform with Anatolian custom — specifically, the custom of placing a curse upon potential violators of the tomb. These monuments are peculiar only in the context of Christian Studies, not in the context of an ancient Anatolian graveyard.

The Christian monuments conventionally have been separated into two broad categories. These categories are defined by the relative directness of the Christian allusions contained in the epitaph. The first category might be labelled "open-expression monuments." Open-expression monuments carry epitaphs which state plainly and explicitly that the deceased and/or dedicant was a Christian. (nos. 2.1, 2.2)

Probably the most famous examples of the open-expression category were prepared exclusively in the highlands of northwestern Phrygia, near Kotiaeion/Kütahya. These monuments displayed a particular, blatant formula: Χριστιανοὶ Χριστιανοῖς, "Christians for Christians." (nos 2.3, 2.4) In addition to the formula, several of the "Christians for Christians" monuments were decorated with a prominently visible cross, carved usually within a stylized, circular wreath at the top of the stone. (no. 2.5) These are among the earliest known examples of the use of the cross symbol by Christians. A rare few of the open-expression epitaphs record the date of dedication, indicating that such openly Christian monuments already were standing in central Anatolia by the middle of the third century. (nos. 2.2, 2.6)

The open-expression category is the smaller by far of the two categories of Anatolian Christian monuments. This circumstance is altogether consistent with the general pattern of Anatolian funerary epigraphy. As previously noted, explicit statements of religious preference were not especially common in the epitaphs either of Anatolian Jews or of adherents of traditional polytheism. Even when present, religious allusions typically were without emphasis and often merely incidental. Nor did the open-expression Christian monuments particularly accentuate the fact of Christianity. The "witness" was brief and seemingly casual — hardly ever going beyond simple mention of the word "Christian." As demonstrated by the selected examples, these Christian epitaphs consisted largely of lists of personal names. A number of the open-expression Christian epitaphs also concluded with the typical Anatolian warning about the consequences of violating the tomb. (no. 2.7)

The second category of Anatolian Christian monuments might be termed "veiled-expression (or crypto-Christian) monuments." This description is not meant here to imply that the "veiling" necessarily was deliberate, although that interpretation (in the past) constituted conventional wisdom. The Christian origin of these monuments simply was not stated directly in the epitaphs, but revealed to us only by miscellaneous clues which appear in the epitaphs and/or in the ornamental stonework. Because clues by their nature must be recognized and interpreted, the Christian origin of any given veiled-expression monument may very well be subject to debate; and the potential debate is made all the more likely by the broad conformity of the Christian monuments to the Anatolian standard.

Some of the clues offered by veiled-expression Christian monuments seem clear enough easily to qualify the monuments for inclusion in the open-expression category. Most significant in this regard are decorative symbols with strong Christian associations. For example, a prominent chi-rho emblem (☧) with A–Ω flanking carved within a decorative pediment at the top of a stele-type tombstone establishes a strong presumption that the burial was Christian. The presumption stands even if the epitaph shows no other Christian characteristic. (no. 2.8) An equally prominent cross has the same effect. (no. 2.9) Every case, however, is not so obvious. Every combined chi-rho and every cross are not necessarily Christian symbols.[1]

In the text of an epitaph from Termessos, ☧ appears apparently as an abbreviation of the title Χρεωφυλάκιον, the city records office. The dedicant

---

[1] The actual purpose of these symbols is open to question. Most commentators have tended to view them as simple confessionary devices, but, especially given the Anatolian concern about protecting the tomb, they may well be hex signs. Note the emperor Constantine's own supposed use of the chi-rho symbol as a protective amulet (Eusebius, *Vita Const.* 31).

certainly was not a Christian, for he stipulated that violators of his tomb would pay a fine to the temple of Zeus Solymos. (no. 2.10)

In the lettering of the texts of several of the "Christians for Christians" epitaphs, the letter chi is tipped on end and becomes ✝. (no. 2.11) Given this specific context, one naturally might suppose that the practice of making chi's into crosses was deliberate and meaningful and "Christian." But examples of the tipped chi are known to occur also in explicitly non-Christian inscriptions, indicating that the chi sometimes was written as a cross only as an artistic convention. Thus the Christian nature of a monument bearing only such a chi-cross and no other supporting characteristic is far from self-evident. (no. 2.12)

Images and expressions phrased in Christian "cult language," compressed into the formulaic medium of the epitaph, and likely mingled there with a variety of traditional elements often render an equally ambiguous product. (no. 2.13) There is a particular danger of confusing Christians with Jews on the basis of vague allusions. (no. 2.14)[2] Yet that is not the limit of possible confusion. One of the most famous of Anatolian epitaphs has been identified both as the epitaph of a Christian bishop of Hieropolis and as the epitaph of a priest of Cybele. (no. 2.15)

As mentioned above, the Christian nature of many veiled-expression monuments is revealed (arguably at least) only because the deceased/dedicant chose to threaten potential violators of the tomb with divine retribution. The Christians, just like their non-Christian neighbors, naturally tended eventually to formulate curses in the terms of their own particular religious beliefs.[3] Probably the most famous Christian curse formula is named, after the Phrygian city where it seems to have originated, the "Eumeneian Formula." The Eumeneian Formula (as conventionally translated) warns the violator of the tomb that he will "reckon with God," ἔσται αὐτῷ πρὸς τὸν Θεόν.[4] (nos. 2.16, 2.17, 2.18, 2.19 et al.)

---

[2] See Ross S. Kraemer, "Jewish Tuna and Christian Fish: Identifying Religious Affiliation in Epigraphic Sources," *Harvard Theological Review* 84 (1991) 141–62.

[3] Christian stoneworkers likely played a key role in this process, and, as such, "Christian" formulae tended to evolve out of formulae which already were in use. For a discussion of a (presumably) Christian stoneyard/workshop which produced monuments bearing the "Christians for Christians" formula see Gary J. Johnson, "A Christian Business and Christian Self-Identity in Third/Fourth Century Phrygia," *Vigiliae Christianae* 48 (1994) 341–66.

[4] A common variant found especially in eastern Phrygia is ἕξει πρὸς τὸν Θεόν. These (and similar) curses may have been presumed to have an active, punitive function. The form(s) are not unlike certain binding spells, which combine various

The Eumeneian Formula is not, of course, an unambiguously Christian formula. Nor does it represent any significant innovation in funerary language. Indeed, we have seen already the use of very similar formulae in both traditional polytheistic and Jewish dedications (nos. 1.16 and 1.20, 1.22, 1.23, 1.24), and nothing about the Eumeneian Formula proper renders it clearly unsuitable for either of those contexts. As such, the claim that the Eumeneian Formula is a "Christian" formula requires some justification. This especially is true because this collection includes a number of epitaphs which are classified as "Christian" epitaphs largely on the basis of their inclusion of the Eumeneian Formula.

The formula's reference to a singular deity is (in general) more apt for Christian or Jewish than for traditional polytheistic usage. Epitaphs of the latter sort did sometimes address singular gods when burials took place in or near the precinct of a particular deity (no. 1.1), but this was a relatively rare occurrence. In addition, a substantial number of epitaphs augment the basic formula in various ways, which seem even less likely to reflect traditional polytheistic religion. For example, God often was described as the "Living God," (no. 2.17) and the confrontation between God and the tomb violator was dated specifically to "Judgment Day."[5]

The major danger in categorizing monuments which bear the Eumeneian Formula is (again) the danger of confusing Christians and Jews. Indeed, such confusion may well be unavoidable, since there is general agreement that both groups probably used the formula. However, Jewish use appears (given our present state of knowledge) to be the exception, and Christian use appears to be the rule.

Virtually every proposed example of Jewish use of the Eumeneian Formula has been predicated solely upon the basis of seemingly Jewish-sounding augmentations of the basic formula (no. 1.24), and these even could be attributed to Jewish converts to Christianity. The formula seems not to appear in any dedication which explicitly cites Jews, Judaism, or Jewish institutions, and does not appear on any monument which carries expressly Jewish symbols like the menorah. The Eumeneian Formula does, on the other hand, occur regularly on monuments which are classifiable as Christian on the basis of additional criteria,

---

verbs with πρός and which (when inscribed upon a lead tablet and placed in a potent location—like a grave) supposedly put the unlucky victim into the power of a deity or spirit. See C.A. Faraone, "The Agonistic Context of Early Greek Binding Spells," in C.A. Faraone and D. Obbink, eds., *Magika Hiera: Ancient Greek Magic and Religion* (Oxford: Oxford University Press, 1991) 3–32.

[5] See, for example, Ramsay, *CB* 2, 514, no. 353.

including explicit mention of Christianity and the presence of Christian symbols and/or terminology. (nos. 2.18, 2.19, 4.2, 4.11, 4.19) In light of these circumstances, there are reasonable grounds for supposing that monuments which carry the Eumeneian Formula are more likely than not to be Christian dedications.

Another notable Christian formula, which appears predominently along a NW-SE axis between Nikaea and Laodikea Katakekaumene, warned the violator of the tomb that he would have to "give an account to God" for his actions: δώσει λόγον τῷ Θεῷ. This formula (perhaps only coincidentally) replicates the phrasing of *Rom.* 14:12: ἄρα οὖν ἕκαστος ἡμῶν περὶ ἑαυτοῦ λόγον δώσει τῷ Θεῷ; "Surely then, each of us, concerning himself, will give account to God."[6] The formula, which appears to be exclusively a Christian usage, is augmented sometimes by reference to "Judgment Day" (nos. 2.20, 4.17); the Judge "of the living and the dead" (no. 4.18), and (like the Eumeneian Formula) appears as well in conjunction with other Christian symbols and/or terminology. (See, for example, nos. 3.12, 4.1: cross; nos. 2.20, 3.10: koimeterion; no. 4.1: Maranatha; no. 4.5: virgins.) The development and use of this formula (and the "Christians for Christians" formula) further document the creation of "Christian" formulae, and (thereby) lend additional implicit support for viewing the Eumeneian Formula also as a Christian product.

---

[6] I owe this reference to Prof. Ludwig Koenen.

(2.1) Marble bomos from Uşak/Akmonia (?).

> Μηνόφιλος καὶ / ἡ γυνὴ αὐτοῦ /
> Αμμια Παιθω ἀ–/ δελφῷ Χρειστι–/
> ανῷ κὲ ᾿Αλεξαν–/ δρία Παιθω ἀν–/
> 4 δρὶ κὲ τὰ παιδία / αὐτῶν μνείας /
> χάριν ἐπύησαν.

2. Αμμια. Native Anatolian personal names which are written in Greek (e.g., Αμμια and Αππη) are now conventionally printed without accent or breathing marks. I have not tried to be consistent regarding this convention, but have followed the practice used in the individual published texts which I have collected and cited.

2–3. ἀδελφῷ Χρειστιανῷ. Whether Paithon is the actual brother of Menophilos or a "brother Christian" is not entirely clear. Given the family focus of the epitaphs, the former is more likely, but cf. no. 2.14.

(2.2) Marble "doorstone" from Uşak/Akmonia (?).

> ῎Ετους τξγ' μη(νὸς) Περειτίου ι'
> Εὐτύχης Εὐτύχου Τατ ι–
> ᾳ γυναικὶ καὶ πατρὶ μνή–
> 4 μης χάριν Χρειστιανο ὶ
> καὶ ἑαυτῷ. Φελλίνας Τημενοθυρ
> ε
> ὶ
> ς

4. Χρειστιανοὶ = Χρειστιανοῖς.

44

(2.1) Marble bomos from Uşak/Akmonia (?).

> Menophilos and his wife,
> Ammia, made (this) for Paithon,
> (his ?) brother, (who was) a Christian;
> and Alexandria, together with
> their children, made (this)
> for Paithon, her husband,
> in memory.

Publication: Gibson, *CFC*, 106, no. 34.

(2.2) Marble "doorstone"[7] from Uşak/Akmonia (?).

> (In the) year 363 (Sullan era = C.E. 278),
> on the 10th day of the month of Pereitios,
> Eutyches, the son of Eutyches, (acquired this)
> for (his) wife Tatia and for (his) father
> and for himself — Christians (all), in memory.
> Phellinas of Temenothyrai (stone mason?).

Publication: Gibson, *CFC*, 108–109, no. 36; W.M. Calder, "Philadelpia and Montanism," *BJRL* 7 (1923) 337, no. 1; *CIG*, no. 38651.

---

[7] A special sort of Phrygian stele carved to resemble a door — the door to the next world.

(2.3) Marble bomos from Abiye.

> Αὐρ(ήλιος) Ζωτικὸς Μαρκι-
> ανὸς τοῖς ἑαυτοῦ γο-
> νεῦσιν ἔτι ζῶν Μαρκί<ω>νι
> 4 κὲ Αππη κὲ ἀδελφῷ ᾿Αρτε-
> μᾷ μνήμης χάριν.
> Χρειστιανοὶ Χρειστιανοῖς.

6. Χρειστιανοὶ. The plural here either is ungrammatical, given the single dedicant, or suggests that the formula refers implicitly to individuals besides those named. Elsa Gibson, *The "Christian For Christians" Inscriptions of Phrygia* (Harvard Theological Studies 32; Missoula, Montana: Scholars Press, 1978) 11, also notes that this line was carved by a different hand than those preceding. For a discussion of the formula's various implications see Gary J. Johnson, "A Christian Business and Christian Self-Identity in Third/Fourth Century Phrygia," *Vigiliae Christianae* 48 (1944) 341–66.

(2.4) Stele from Alibey.

> Αὐρ(ηλία) Κύριλλα / ἀνδρὶ ᾿Ασκληπ–/
> <ι>άδη κὲ ἑαυτῇ ζῶ–/ σα κὲ τὰ τέκνα
> <α>ὐ–/ τῶν ᾿Ασκληπι–/ άδης πατρὶ
> 4 κὲ / μητρὶ κὲ Δόμν–/ α νύνφη ἐκυροῖς /
> Χρηστια–/νοὶ Χρησ–/ τιανοῖς, /
> μνήμης χ–/ άριν.

2. τέκνα either is an incorrect plural or is meant to refer both to the son and to Domna, the daughter-in-law.

4. νύνφη = νύμφη.

5. Χρηστιανοὶ. This spelling of "Christian" is by far more common in the epitaphs than either Χριστιανοὶ or Χρειστιανοὶ.

(2.3) Marble bomos from Abiye.

> Aurelios Zotikos Markianos,
> (acquired this) while still living
> for his parents Markion and
> Appe and for his brother, Artemas,
> in memory.
> Christians for Christians.

Publication: Gibson, *CFC*, 11, no. 2; W.M. Calder, "Philadephia and Montanism," *BJRL* 7 (1923) 337, no. 3.

(2.4) Stele from Alibey.

> Aurelia Kyrilla, (acquired this) while still living
> for (her) husband Asklepiadesand for herself;
> and their children, Asklepiades (the son of
> Asklepiades, dedicated this) to (his) father;
> and Domna, the bride (of Asklepiades, dedicated
> this) to (her) parents-in-law.
> Christians for Christians, in memory.

Publication: Gibson, *CFC*, 32, no. 14; W.M. Calder, "Leaves from an Anatolian Notebook," *BJRL* 13 (1929) 268, no. 1.

(2.5) Marble stele from Gediz (?).

✝

Αὐρ(ήλιος) Εἰστρατόνι-
κος τέκνῳ Ἐρπι-
δηφόρῳ κὲ Διονυσ-
4 ᾳς ἀνδρὶ κὲ τὰ τέ-
κνα αὐτῶν Εἰστρα-
τόνικος κὲ Κύρ-
ιλος κὲ Πατρίκις
8 κὲ Φίλητος πατρ-
ὶ, Χρησσιανοὶ Χρ-
ησσιανῷ.

1–2, 5–6. Εἰστρατόνικος. Prothetic ι or ει before σ occurs commonly in Anatolian epitaphs. Cf. no. 2.16, line 7 (τῇ ἰστήλῃ) and no. 4.5, line 4 (τὴν ἰστήλ(η)ν]). See A. Wilhelm, "Griechische Grabinschriften aus Kleinasien," *SBBerlin* (1932) 802–03.

2–3. Ἐρπιδηφόρῳ. Alternation of λ and ρ in names beginning ἐλπιδ- is discussed by Jean and Louis Robert, *Bulletin épigraphique* 72 (1959) 161; 74 (1961) 315.

9–10. Χρησσιανοὶ Χρησσιανῷ. For a discussion of the assimilation of τ after σ see W. Tabbernee, *New Documents Illustrating Early Christianity* 3 (North Ryde, N.S.W., Australia: Macquarie University, 1983) 130.

(2.5) Marble stele from Gediz (?).

Aurelios Eistratonikos
(acquired this) for (his) son
Erpidephoros; and Dionysas
(dedicated this) to her husband;
and their children, Eistratonikos
and Kyrilos and Patrikis
and Philetos, (dedicated this)
to (their) father, Christians for a Christian.

Publication: Gibson, *CFC*, 22, no. 9.

(2.6) Bomos from Altintaş.

[τ]λγ'/ Χρειστιανοὶ / Χρειστιανο[ῖς] /
Αὐρ(ηλία) Αμμεια / σὺν τῷ γαμβρ[ῷ] /
αὐτῶν Ζωτι– / κῷ κὲ σὺν τοῖ[ς] /
4   ἐγόνοις αὐτῶ[ν] / ᾽Αλλεξανδρείᾳ /
κὲ Τελεσφόρῳ / κὲ ᾽Αλλεξάνδρῳ /
συνβίῳ ἐποίη– / σαν.

1. Χρειστιανο[ῖς]. The reading of the final three letters is not completely sure. If correct, either the plural is ungrammatical or intended to refer to the dedicants as well as the deceased.

5. κὲ. Gibson, *CFC*, 57, suggests that the inclusion of this word is a mistake, and that Allexandros is the name of the husband rather than a third grandchild.

(2.7) Marble bomos from Aykirikçi.

᾽Ενθάδε γῆ κατέχι Σωσθ[έ]–
νην ἄνδρα ποθητὸν
καὶ κάλλι καὶ με<γέ>θι καῖ σ[ω]–
4   φροσύνῃ δὲ μάλιστα, τὸ–
ν πάσης ἀρετῆς καὶ ἐν
ἄνδρεσι κῦδος ἔχοντ–
α. τριάκοντα ἐτῶν ἔ–
8   θανον, λύπησα δὲ πά–
ντας, καὶ πενθεροὺς [λύ]–
πησα, ψυχὴν δὲ ἐμάρα[ν]–

(2.6) Bomos from Altıntaş.

> (In the year) 333 (Sullan era = C.E. 248),
> Christians for Christians,
> Aurelia Ammeia,
> along with their son-in-law, Zotikos,
> and with their grandchildren,
> Allexandreia and Telesphoros,
> for (her) husband, Allexandros,
> made (this).

Publication: *NewDocs* 3, 131; Gibson, *CFC*, 56, no. 22; W.H. Buckler, W.M. Calder, and C.W.M. Cox, "Asia Minor 1924. Monuments from the Upper Tembris Valley," *JRS* 18 (1928) 21f, no. 231; W.M. Calder, "Philadephia and Montanism," *BJRL* 7 (1923) 337, no. 2.

(2.7) Marble bomos from Aykirikçi.

> Here earth covers Sosthenes,
> a man sorely-missed for
> his beauty and greatness and
> especially for his self-control,
> who was excellent in every way and
> renowned among men; I died
> at age 30, giving grief to all,
> and giving grief to my in-laws; and

α γυνηκὸς μετὰ ἧς τ[ρί]–
12 α ἔτη συνέζησα, ἀπὸ
ἧς ἓν τέκνον ἔσχον. ο[ἱ]
δὲ γονῖς πρὸ ἐμοῦ ἐν–
θάδε κῖντη. ᾿Αλέξανδ–
16 ρος πρεσβύτερος μετὰ
τῆς συνβίου Αππης κα[ὶ]
τῆς θυγατρὸς Κυρίλλης
καὶ τῆς ἐγγόνης Δόμ[ν]–
20 ης τοῖς συτέκνοις Σω–
σθᾷ καὶ Δόμνῃ και Σωσ–
θένῃ γάνβρῷ γλυκυτά–
τῳ ἐποίαισαν χάριν, Χ–
24 ρηστιανοὶ Χρηστιανοῖ[ς].
τὸν Θεόν σοι ἀναγν[ο]–
ὺς μὴ ἀδικαίσις.

1. ᾿Ενθάδε γῆ κατέχι ...This phrase begins a substantial number of metrical epitaphs, providing thereby further evidence of the use of poetic phrasebooks to build epitaphs. See additional examples in Gibson, *CFC*, 85f, and cf. no. 4.16.

16. πρεσβύτερος. Presumably this refers to the Christian ecclesiastical office.

20. συτέκνοις = συντέκνοις. See Gibson, *CFC*, 35, for additional examples of ν deleted before a dental. The translation "fellow-parents" was suggested to me by William Tabbernee. Sosthas and Domna seem most likely to be the deceased parents of Sosthenes and, thus, "fellow-parents" to his in-laws.

25–26. τὸν Θεόν ...ἀδικαίσις. Regarding this formulaic imprecation, see Gibson, *CFC*, 62ff. The same curse appears also on explicitly non-Christian dedications in northwestern Phrygia.

I made to wither the spirit of my wife,

with whom I lived together 3 years,

(and) from whom I had one child.

(My) parents lie here before me.

Alexandros, a presbyter, with

(his) wife, Appe, and (their) daughter,

Kyrilla, and (their) granddaughter,

Domna, for (their) fellow-parents,

Sosthas and Domna, and for

Sosthenes, (their) dearest son-in-law,

made (this) in memory,

Christians for Christians.

By God, do not abuse (the tomb)!

Publication: Gibson, *CFC*, 76ff, no. 28; W.M.Calder, "Philadelphia and Montanism," *BJRL* 7 (1923) 339–40, no. 8; G. Mendel, "Catalogue du Musée de Brousse," *BCH* 33 (1909) 420ff, no. 427.

(2.8) Marble stele from Perinthos-Herakleia (Thrace).

A ☧ Ω

Αὐρ(ήλιος) Μάρκελλος Δι–
ογένους Ἡρακλεώ–
της πολίτης φυλ–
4 ῆς ἔκτης κατεσκ–
ευάσατο λατό {λατ}-
μιν ἐμαυτῷ κὲ τῇ γ–
λυκυτάτῃ μου γυνε–
8 κὶ Αὐρ(ηλίᾳ) Ἀρτεμιδώρᾳ καὶ
τοῖς τέκνοις μου· ἴ τις
ἕτερον τολμήσι καταθέσθε,
δώ[σ]ι τῇ πόλι προστίμου χ–
12 άριν ✳ μύ(ρια) αφ'· εἰ δέ τις κακου–
ργήσι τοῦτο λατόμιν, ὀρφα–
νὰ τέκνα λίποιτο γυνέκα τε
χήραν, ἐν πυρὶ πάντα δράμ–
16 οιτο, κακῶν ὑπόχιρος ὀλῖτε.
χέροις π[α]ροδῖτα.

5–6, 13. λατόμιν = λατόμ(ε)ιν. This word (meaning "stone-quarry") is unusual as a desigation of the tomb.

13–15. ὀρφανὰ...ὀλῖτε. Cf. the curses in nos. 1.1 and 1.10.

(2.8) Marble stele from Perinthos-Herakleia (Thrace).

A ☧ Ω

I, Aurelios Markellos, the son
of Diogenes, a citizen of
Herakleia, of the 6th phyle,
constructed this stone-tomb
for myself and for my
dearest wife, Aurelia Artemidora,
and for my children. If anyone
should undertake to bury another (here),
he will, on that account, pay to
the city as a fine 1500 x 10,000 denarii.
If anyone should harm this tomb,
he will leave behind orphaned children
and a bereaved wife.
He will run totally in fire; he will
die under the hand of evil men.
Farewell passersby.

Publication: E. Kalinka, "Antiken zu Perinth," *Jahreshefte des Österreichischen Archäologischen Institutes in Wien* 1 (1898) Beiblatt, col. 112 f, no. 10.

(2.9) Limestone stele from Ladik/Laodikea Katakekaumene

✝

Αὐρ(ήλιος) Παπας
υεἰὸς Παύλου
Σουμνηνὸς ἀνέ[σ]–
4 τησα τῇ συνβίου
μου καὶ ἑαυτῷ
ζῶν καὶ τοῖς
τέκνοις μου μν[ή]–
8 μνης χάριν.

✝

(2.10) Sarcophagus from Termessos.

...Μάρεινος Ἑρμαίου ἐσημιώσατο ἐπὶ
τοῦ ✝ ὅτι ἐν τῇ οὔσῃ σόρῳ...
μηδενὸς ἔχοντος ἐξουσίαν καταθέσθαι
4 εἰς αὐτὴν ἕτερον σκῆνος...

(2.9) Limestone stele from Ladik/Laodikea Katakekaumene

+

I, Aurelios Papas,

the son of Paulos,[8]

(a resident?) of Soumna,[9]

erected (this) for

my wife and for myself,

while still living, and

for my children,

in memory.

+

Publication: *MAMA* 1, no. 213.

(2.10) Sarcophagus from Termessos.

... Mareinos, the son of Hermaios,

signified at the Chr(eophylakeion) that

in his own sarcophagus ... no one has

the authority to bury in it another

body....[10]

Publication: K.G. Lanckoronski, *Städte Pamphyliens und Pisidiens* 2 (Vienna: F. Temsky, 1892) 219, no. 173.

---

[8] Personal names sometimes provide additional hints concerning religious affiliation. By the fourth century, at least, Christians increasingly began to utilize names drawn from scripture or expressing Christian virtues.

[9] Perhaps a village of Laodikea Katakekaumene.

[10] The epitaph is lengthy and full presentation would serve no purpose here. The warning against violation is very similar to that of no. 1.16, also from Termessos.

(2.11) Marble bomos from Yalnizsaray.

Αὐρ(ήλιος) Εὔτυ┼ος Μενάνδ[ρου]
κὲ Πρόκλα τέκνῳ Κυρίλλῳ κὲ [νύ]–
μφη Δόμνη κὲ ἐγγόνῳ Κυριακῷ
4 καταλιπόντες τέκνα ὀρφανὰ
'Αλέξανδρον κὲ Πρόκλαν κὲ Αὐ[ρ(ήλιος)]
Εὔτυχος ἀδελφῷ Κυρίλλῳ κὲ ἐνα–
τρὶ Δόμνη κὲ Εὐτυ┼ιανῆς δαέρι
8 [Κ]υρίλλῳ κὲ ἐνατρὶ Δόμνῃ.
┼ρησ–
τιανοὶ ┼ρησ–
τιανοῖς

4. καταλιπόντες should follow Κυρίλλῳ *et al.* in the dative.

6–7, 8. ἐνατρὶ. Gibson, *CFC*, p. 13, notes that this word takes two meanings here: "brother's wife" and "wife of husband's brother."

(2.12) Limestone bomos from Kadin Khan/Laodikea
Katakekaumene.

Αὐ(ρήλιος) Διονύσιο[ς Μ]–
ανῃ πατρὶ κα[ὶ]
Παύλῃ μητρ[ὶ ζ]–
4 <ώ>σῃ ἀνέστησ–
εν μνήμης ┼ά–
ριν.

(2.11) Marble bomos from Yalnizsaray.

> Aurelios Eutychos, the son of Menandros,
> and (his wife) Prokla (erected this)
> for their child Kyrillos and (his)
> bride, Domna, and for their grandson
> Kyriakos, who leave behind as orphaned
> children Alexandros and Prokla; and
> Aurelios Eutychos (the Younger dedicated
> this) for (his) brother, Kyrillos, and for
> his sister-in-law, Domna, and Eutychianes,
> (the wife of Aurelios Eutychos the Younger,
> dedicated this) for her brother-in-law,
> Kyrillos, and for her sister-in-law, Domna.
> Christians for Christians

Publication: *NewDocs* 3, 133–34; Gibson, *CFC*, 12, no. 3.

(2.12) Limestone bomos from Kadin Khan/Laodikea Katakekaumene.

> Aurelios Dionysios
> erected this for his father, Manes,
> and for his mother, Paula,[11] who
> is still living, in memory.

Publication: *MAMA* 1, no. 154; W.M. Calder, "Studies in Early Christian Epigraphy: II," *JRS* 14 (1924) 91, no. 10.

---

[11] This name may lend further credence to interpreting the chi-cross in l.5 as a Christian symbol.

(2.13) Bomos from Kelendres/Hieropolis.

['Εκ]λεκτὴς πό[λε]ως ὁ πολεί[της τ]οῦτ' ἐποί[ησα] /
[ζῶν, ἵ]ν' ἔχω φανε[ρῶς] σώματος ἔνθα θέσιν. /
οὔνομα 'Αλέξανδρος 'Αντωνίου μαθητὴς ποιμένος
4 ἁγνοῦ. / οὐ μέντοι τύμβῳ τις ἐμῷ ἕτερόν τινα
θήσει· / εἰ δ' οὖν, 'Ρωμαίων ταμειῷ θήσει
δισχείλια χρυσά / καὶ χρηστῇ πατρίδι 'Ιεροπόλει
χείλια χρυσά. / ἐγράφη ἔτει τ' μηνὶ ς'· ζόντος. /
8 εἰρήνη παράγουσιν καὶ μνησκομένοις περὶ ἡμῶν.

2. θέσιν (θέσις). This word (here designating simply "a place") later evolved into a Christian term for "tomb."

4. τύμβῳ (τύμβος) was used widely in Anatolia as a general term for "tomb," appearing most commonly in metrical inscriptions. See Kubinska, *Les Monuments*, 25ff.

8. εἰρήνη. The bestowal of "peace" is a very characteristic Christian blessing. See no. 2.14 following and also the large number of (apparently) Christian dedications from Rome which use the formula, *in pacem* — discussed by Graydon F. Snyder, *Ante Pacem* (Macon, Georgia: Mercer University Press, 1985) 127ff.

8. μνησκομένοις may refer only to remembering or acknowledging the deceased, but likely includes abiding by the prohibition against interring another body in the tomb.

(2.13) Bomos from Kelendres/Hieropolis.

> I, the citizen of an elect city, made this, while
> still living, so that I would have, manifestly,
> a place here for my body. My name is
> Alexandros, son of Antonios, a disciple of the Holy
> Shepherd.[12] No one indeed will put another (body) in my
> tomb. If consequently (anyone should do so),
> he will pay 2000 gold (coins) to the Roman fiscus
> and 1000 gold (coins) to (my) good native city,
> Hieropolis. (This) was written (by me).
> while still living, in the year 300 (Sullan era =
> C.E. 215) in the 6th month.
> Peace upon you who pass and pay heed.

Publication: Ramsay, *CB* 2, 720, no. 656.

---

[12] Cf. the opening lines of no. 2.15. Ramsay, *CB* 2, 724, suggests that the "elect city" is not really Hieropolis, but "the heavenly city."

(2.14) Bomos from Maghajil/The Pentapolis

Αὐρ(ήλιος) Διονοί–
σιος πρεσβ[ύ]–
τερος ζῶν κα–
4 τεσκεύασεν
τὸ κοιμητήρι–
ον. Εἰρήνη πᾶσι
τοῖς ἀδελφο–
8   ῖς

5. κοιμητήριον = "sleeping place" used as a designation for the tomb seems primarily to have been a Christian invention/usage. Cf. no. 2.20 *et al.*, and see note no. 13 following.

(2.14) Bomos from Maghajil/The Pentapolis.

> Aurelios Dionoisios,
>> a presbyter,
>> while still living,
>> constructed this koimeterion.
>> Peace to all the brothers.[13]

Publication: Ramsay, *CB* 2, 719, no. 654.

---

[13] This probably is a Christian dedication. Presbyter is a Christian office, *koimeterion* predominantly a Christian usage, and εἰρήνη a typical Christian blessing. On the other hand, presbyter also is a Jewish office. A few examples of clearly Jewish use of *koimeterion* are known, and see J.B. Frey, *Corpus Inscriptionum Judaicarum* (2 vols.; Rome: Pontificio Istituto di Archeologia Cristiana, 1936–1952) 2 no. 800, a Jewish dedication from the vicinity of Constantinople (a menorah is carved on the stone) which ends with the blessing εἰρήνη, "peace."

EARLY-CHRISTIAN EPITAPHS FROM ANATOLIA

(2.15) Marble bomos (fragmented) from Hieropolis.

Ἐκλεκτῆς πόλεως ὁ πολείτης τοῦτ' ἐποίησα
ζῶν, ἵν' ἔχω φανερῶς σώματος ἔνθα θέσιν,
οὔνομ' Ἀβέρκιος ὤν, ὁ μαθητὴς ποιμένος ἁγνοῦ,
4 ὃς βόσκει προβάτων ἀγέλας ὄρεσιν πεδίοις τε
ὀφθαλμοὺς ὃς ἔχει, μεγάλους πάντη καθορῶντας
οὗτος γάρ μ' ἐδίδαξε [τὰ ζωῆς] γράμματα πιστά.
εἰς Ῥώμην ὃς ἔπεμψεν ἔμεν βασιλῆαν ἀθρῆσαι
8 καὶ βασίλισσαν ἰδεῖν χρυσόστολον χρυσοπέδιλον·

(2.15) Marble bomos (fragmented) from Hieropolis.[14]

> I, the citizen of an elect city, made this,
>
> while still living, so that I would have,
>
> manifestly, a place here for my body.
>
> My name, indeed, is Aberkios, a disciple of the
>
> Holy Shepherd, who pastures his flocks of sheep
>
> in the mountains and the plains, and who has
>
> powerful eyes looking down everywhere.
>
> For this (Shepherd) taught me the trustworthy knowledge of
>
> life. (It was he) who dispatched me to Rome to
>
> observe the kingdom[15] and see the queen
>
> in the golden robe and golden sandals.[16]
>
> Indeed, I saw a people there (who were) marked
>
> with an illustrious Seal, and I saw the
>
> plain of Syria and all the cities, having

---

[14] Only that part of the text which is underlined is visible on the surviving fragments. The remainder of the text depends upon a copy of the epitaph made by the author of a "Life of Aberkios" which is preserved in the *Acta Sanctorum* and upon comparison to no. 2.13, which seems to borrow the opening and closing formulae of the Aberkios epitaph. The words in the brackets are conjectural reconstructions of lacunae in the manuscripts, all of which were proposed by nineteenth century editors. Aberkios supposedly died ca. 192.

[15] This line has sparked considerable controversy, but I take it to mean that Aberkios was to observe the "kingdom," i.e. the Roman Empire, as he travelled around. He stresses the breadth of his travels in the following lines, travels that take him from the center of the empire all the way to the eastern frontier, i.e. "across the Euphrates."

[16] The "queen" presumably is the city of Rome.

λαὸν δ᾽ εἶδον ἐκεῖ λαμπρὰν σφράγειδαν ἔχοντα
καὶ Συρίης πέδον εἶδον καὶ ἄστεα παντὰ Νίσιβιν
Εὐφράτην διαβὰς πάντῃ δ᾽ ἔσχον συνομήθεις·
12 Παῦλον ἔχων ἐπό[μην], πίστις πάντῃ δὲ προυῆγε,
καὶ παρέθηκε τροφὴν πάντῃ ἰχθὺν ἀπὸ πηγῆς
πανμεγέθη, καθαρὸν ὃν ἐδράξατο παρθένος ἁγνή,
καὶ τοῦτο ἐπέδωκε φίλοις ἐσθέειν διὰ παντὸς /
16 οἶνον χρηστὸν ἔχουσα κέρασμα δίδουσα μετ᾽
ἄρτου. / ταῦτα παρεστὼς εἶπον Ἀβέρκιος ὧδε
γραφῆναι· / ἑβδομηκοστὸν ἔτος καὶ δεύτερον ἦγον
ἀληθῶς / ταῦθ᾽ ὁ νοῶν εὔξαιτο ὑπὲρ [Ἀβερκίου] πᾶς
20 ὁ συνῳδός. / οὐ μέντοι τύμβῳ τις ἐμῷ ἕτερόν
τινα θήσει· / εἰ δ᾽ οὖν Ῥωμαίων ταμειῷ θήσει
δισχείλια χρυσά / καὶ χρηστῇ πατρίδι
Ἱεροπόλει χείλια χρυσά.

16. χρηστὸν. Given the number of epitaphs in which "Christian" is spelled with η, this adjective often (in Christian dedications) has the potential to carry theological significance. Note, for example, Gibson, *CFC*, 71, no. 27, where an anonymous dedicant (who claims to have authored the epitaph) refers to himself as φιλοχρήστωρ, "lover of Christos/Chrestos?" The epitaph includes the "Christians for Christians" formula-also spelled with η.

crossed the Nisibisian[17] Euphrates (and)
everywhere, indeed, I had companions; having
Paul, I followed after (and) faith everywhere
led the way, and everywhere laid food
before me: fish from the source,
beyond measure (and) spotless, which a
Holy Virgin seized, and she gave this (food)
bountifully to friends to eat always,
having a good wine and giving (it) diluted, with bread.
I, Aberkios, being nearby, dictated these things
to be written down here. Truly, I was
celebrating (my) seventy-second year.
May he who understands these (words) and
everyone who agrees pray for the sake of Aberkios.
However, no one will put another (body)
in my tomb. If consequently (anyone should
do so), he will pay 2000 gold (coins) to the Roman fiscus
and 1000 gold (coins) to (my)
good native city, Hieropolis.

Publication: *NewDocs* 6, 177–81, no. 26; W. Wischmeyer, "Die Aberkiosinschrift als Grabepigramm," *Jahrbuch für Antike und Christentum* 23 (1980) 22ff; Graydon F. Snyder, *Ante Pacem: Archaeological Evidence of Church Life Before Constantine* (Macon, Georgia: Mercer University Press, 1985) 139–40; Ramsay, *CB* 2, 722ff, no. 657.

---

[17] Nisibis is a city near the Euphrates, on the frontier between the Roman Empire and Persia.

(2.16) Stele from Cepni köy.

> Αὐρ(ηλία) Νανα Μηνοφίλου
> κατεσκεύασεν τὸ
> μνημῖον τῷ υἱῷ Εὐ–
> 4 φήμῳ ἐκ τῶν ἀπολει–
> φθέντων ὑπὸ αὐτοῦ
> ὑπαρχόντων·
> ὃς ταύτῃ τῇ ἰστήλῃ
> 8 κακοεργέα χεῖρα
> προσοίσι, ἔστη αὐτῷ
> πρὸς τὸν Θεόν.

9. ἔστη. η (as well as ε) replaces αι in the epitaphs. Cf. no. 4.16, 1.4: ἤσιον = αἴσιον.

(2.16) Stele from Cepni köy.

> Aurelia Nana, the daughter of Menophilos,
> constructed this memorial
> for (her) son Euphemos
> out of the assets of an inheritance
> which were left behind by him;
> whoever should lay evil-doing
> hands on this stele
> will reckon with God.

Publication: W.M. Calder, "Early-Christian Epitaphs from Phrygia," *AS* 5 (1955) 36, no. 5.

(2.17) Marble bomos from Ishikli/Eumeneia.

> Αὐρ(ηλία) Πρόκλα
> κατεσκεύασεν
> τὸ ἡρῷον αὐτῇ καὶ
> 4 τῷ ἀνδρὶ καὶ τοῖς
> τέκνοις Φιλίππῳ
> καὶ Παυλίνῃ μνή–
> [μη]ς χάριν· εἰ δέ
> 8 [τις] ἐπιχιρήσει
> [θεῖ]ναι ἕτερον
> [ἔ]σται αὐτῷ πρὸς
> τὸν Θεὸν τὸν / ζῶντα.

3. ἡρῷον (originally meaning the "shrine of a hero") was a widely-used, general term for "tomb" in Anatolia. In Phrygia, the term was particularly prominent at Eumeneia. The translation "shrine" has been maintained here.

(2.18) Limestone block from near Dinar.

> Χριστιανοί
>
> Καπίτω[ν- - - -ca. 16 - - - -ἐ]πόησα τὸ ἡ–
> ρῷον [ἐμαυτ]ῷ καὶ τῇ [γυναικί ? μου- - ca. 8 - -]
> 4 [καὶ τῇ ἀδ]ελφῇ μου Τροφίμῃ· εἰ δ[έ τις ἕ]–
> τερος [ἐπ]ιτηδεύσει ἔσται αὐτῷ πρ[ὸς] τὸν
> Θεόν.

(2.17) Marble bomos from Ishikli/Eumemeia

> Aurelia Prokla
> constructed this shrine
> for herself and for
> her husband and for
> their children, Philippos
> and Paulina,[18] in memory;
> if anyone should attempt
> to inter another (here),
> he will reckon with the Living God.

Publication: *MAMA* 4, no. 359; Ramsay, *CB* 2, 529, no. 374.

(2.18) Limestone block from near Dinar.

> Christians

> I, Kapiton . . . made this my shrine (for myself)
> and for (my wife?) . . . (and for) my
> sister, Trophima; if any other should try
> (to inter someone else) he will
> reckon with God.

Publication: Gibson, *CFC*, 112, no. 39; *MAMA* 6, no. 235.

---

[18] Note again names with *New Testament* connections — by themselves insignificant, but reassuring when categorizing a monument as "Christian" only on the basis of the Eumeneian Formula.

(2.19) Limestone (?) block from near Dinar.

ΖΩΕΠΔ ☧ ΧΧΡΕΙ

Αὐρή(λιος) Οὐάλης β΄ ταυρεινᾶς
κατασκευάσα {ς} τὸ ἡρῷον
4 ἐμαυτῷ καὶ τῇ συνζύγῳ Λου-
λιανῇ κὲ τοῖς κειμένοις
μετὰ ὑμῶν· εἰ δὲ θέλῃ τεις
οἰστέα βαρῆσ<ε> ἔσται αὐτῷ
8 π(ρ)ὸς τὸν ἐξουσειάζοτα πάσης ψυχῆς· μή τεις ἀνύ-
ξεις· ὁ ὅρος μέγα<ς> εἰστί.

ὃς ἂν
12 ὀστέον ἔ-
νθω βά-
λῃ ποτὲ
ἔξω ἔστε
16 αὐτῷ πρὸς
τὸν Θεόν.

4. συνζύγῳ is an unusual substitute for the more typical, συμβίῳ.

72

(2.19) Limestone (?) block from near Dinar.

ΖΩΕΠΔ ⳨ XXPEI[19]

I, Aurelios Ouales the Younger, a shoemaker,
constructed this shrine
for myself and for my wife, Louliana,
and for those (children?) who lie with us;
if anyone should wish to weight
down (our) bones (by inserting another body),
he will reckon with him who has authority
over every soul; none of you should
open (this tomb)! The boundary
(between life and death) is great.

Whoever should
throw a bone out from here
at any time
will reckon with God.

Publication: Gibson, *CFC*, 113, no. 40; *MAMA* 6, no. 234.

---

[19] The full meaning of these letters is obscure, but the XXREI likely stands for Χ(ρειστιανοὶ) Χρει(στιανοῖς), "Christians for Christians."

(2.20) Stele from Akçapinar/Nikaea.

Αὐρ(ήλιος) Χρύσανθος κατεσ

                        κ

  τὸ κοιμητήριν ἐμαυ–   ε

  τῷ κὲ τῇ γλυκυτάτῃ   ὑ

4 μου συνβίῳ Βαλερίᾳ   α

  κὲ τοῖς πενθεροῖς   σ

  μου Αὐρηλίῳ Ἀντιόχῳ   α

  κὲ τῇ συνβίῳ αὐτοῦ Ἀ–

8 φροδισίᾳ Αὐρηλίαι

  κὲ τοῖς γλυκυτάτοις

  αὐτῶ<ν> ἐγγόνοις

  ἰς τὸ χαρισθὲν ἡμ–

12 ῖν παρασπόριν

  ὑπὸ Αὐρ(ηλίου) Ἀγελίου.

  εἴ τις δὲ σκύλῃ τὸ

  κοιμητήριν, ὁ

16 ἄνομως δώσι

  λόγο<ν> Θεῷ ἐν ἡ–

  μέρᾳ κρίσεως

  κὲ τῷ ταμίῳ ✳ ρ'. / χέρετε.

2. κοιμητήριν = κοιμητήριον.

12. παρασπόριν = παρασπόριον.

14. σκύλῃ (σκυλεύω). This verb (usually meaning "to strip a dead enemy of arms") was widely used in the territory of Nikaea to describe violation of the tomb.

16. ἄνομως = ἄνομος.

(2.20) Stele from Akçapinar/Nikaea.

> I, Aurelios Chrysanthos, constructed
> this koimeterion for myself,
> for my dearest wife Baleria,
> for my in-laws, Aurelios Antiochos
> and his wife, Aphrodisia Aurelia,
> and for their beloved grandchildren
> in the *parasporion*[20] graciously
> given to us by Aurelios Agelios.
> If anyone should violate the
> koimeterion, the lawbreaker will
> give account to God on Judgment Day
> and pay the treasury 100 denarii.
> Farewell.

Publication: Şahin, *Iznik* 1, no. 555.

---

[20] This apparently denotes a parcel of land. See Louis Robert, *Bulletin épigraphique* (1980) 516.

CHAPTER 3

CHRISTIAN SOCIAL STATUS AND OCCUPATIONS

The Christian funerary monuments/epitaphs provide a certain amount of information concerning the social and economic circumstances of Christians in Roman Anatolia. This information cannot be described as "detailed," but is often very interesting. Particularly useful are those monuments which help to illuminate the ill-documented period in Christian history preceding the conversion of the emperor Constantine and his legitimation of the Christian religion in C.E. 312. Accordingly, a number of the monuments selected for presentation in this chapter are pre-Constantinian. None of them (probably) dates from later than the fourth century. However, the issue of dating is potentially controversial. Few of the monuments are explicitly dated. Determination of the date of dedication (as perhaps even the identification of Christian origin) often depends upon the interpretation of clues: nomenclature (see p. 5), lettering/artistic style, vocabulary and formulae, etc. No comprehensive defense of the dating of the monuments has been possible in this context.

The epitaphs suggest that Christians were present at the highest levels of the social hierarchy in some cities of Anatolia long before the time of Constantine.[1] These Christians include the chief magistrate of a moderate-sized Bithynian city (no. 3.1) and several individuals who identify themselves as members of a civic *boule* = city council in Phrygia. (nos. 3.2, 3.3, 3.4, 3.5, 3.6, 3.7)[2] Membership in the *boule* was restricted generally to families of wealth and/or local status. However, one must acknowledge that the cities in question were neither very large nor particularly important. Nor, for that matter, are the monuments themselves very elaborate. How these central Anatolian aristocrats would compare to their counterparts in the larger coastal

---

[1] This circumstance, of course, is not very surprising. The presence of Roman citizens among those Christians prosecuted by Pliny the Younger in Bithynia-Pontos ca. 110–112 probably carries the same implication. See Gary J. Johnson, "*De conspiratione delatorum*: Pliny and the Christians Revisited," *Latomus* 47:2 (1988) 417–22.

[2] Ramsay, *CB* 2, 519 (commenting upon no. 3.2) notes also one Papylos of Thyateira, a Christian of the time of Marcus Aurelius, who (according to the *Acta Carpi*) was reported to the Roman proconsul because he was a member of the *boule*.

cities or in the other major cities of the empire is unclear. But one of them, at least, managed to marry into the family of a Roman senator. (no. 3.5)

Membership in the *boule* also was hereditary and mandatory. Nevertheless, the mention of this and other civic offices in the epitaphs suggests that these Christian councilors were both conscious of and prideful of their positions, and not at all bothered by their political entanglements. This seems particularly to be the case since nos. 3.2 – 3.7 were all prepared by the dedicants themselves before their own deaths. For the most part, so far as we can tell, being Christians seems not to have altered their careers, interests, and/or values to any appreciable degree. (cf. no. 3.8) Pride in the family and in worldly attainments shines through even in the one example where loyalty to Christianity did prompt a career change. (no. 3.5) Two of our sample even demonstrate a rather surprising apparent willingness to participate in events associated with the imperial cult and/or the traditional gods. (nos. 3.1, 3.4)

Perhaps predictably, in light of the preceding examples, Christians are found also employed in the imperial service, and at various levels which correspond to the dispersal of Christians in civilian society. One of the aristocrats began his career as an officer (presumably) in the *officium* of a provincial governor (no. 3.5), and other literal Christian soldiers appear in a variety of billets/job specialties. (nos. 3.9, 3.10, 3.11, 3.12, 4.4, 4.11)

Another of the councilors cited above describes himself as a "physician" (no. 3.6), and the epitaphs reveal Christians also in a variety of other civilian occupations, which would have demanded various levels of skill and/or education and which no doubt commanded various amounts of respect. As alluded to previously (p. 41), the very existence of the Christian monuments probably documents the presence of Christian stoneworkers. Other occupations cited include: lawyer (no. 4.12), shoemaker (no. 2.19), merchant (no. 3.13), wood carver (no. 3.14), baker (no. 3.15), goldsmith (no. 3.16), and orchard keeper (no. 3.17).

The dedicant of no. 3.18 was apparently a butcher. The epitaph itself does not state that fact, but a large cleaver is carved under the inscription. Therein lies a point. Sometimes the mute testimony of the ornamental carving on the gravestone can be almost as informative as words. Because of such decoration we happen to know that the aristocratic dedicant of no. 3.4 was an athlete. The gravestone of the wood carver is decorated with the images of a hammer and chisel, and several of the "Christians for Christians" monuments presented in the previous chapter are decorated with images of oxen and agricultural implements. (nos. 2.3, 2.4, 2.5, 2.11)

Because early Christianity seems primarily to have been an urban religion which, in most areas, took a long time to penetrate the countryside, the agricultural motifs on these "Christians for Christians" monuments are especially interesting. The monuments are handsome and surely expensive. Whatever might have been the circumstances of the dedicants, they were not penniless peasants. And that really is what all the Christians in this book have in common — a level of income sufficient to afford some kind of stone burial monument. There also must have been Christians who were not so fortunate, and who, consequently, have left of themselves no trace.

(3.1) Limestone column from Bolu/Bithynion-Klaudiopolis.[3]

Τοῖς ἁγνοτάτοις καὶ .
Θεῷ πιστεύσασιν Μάρ[κῳ]
Δημητριανῷ τῷ α' ἄρξαν–
4 τ{ο}ι καὶ πάντα πολειτευσα–
μένῳ, ἀγωνοθετήσαντι δὲ
ἐπιτείμως, καὶ τῇ γλυκυτάτῃ
μητρὶ Αὐ(ρηλία) Παννυχίδι Αὐρ(ηλία)
8 Δημητριανὴ θυγάτηρ αὐτῶν
[κ]αὶ ὁ γαμβρὸς Δομ(ίτιος) ῾Ηλιόδωρος
ἅμ[α] καὶ τῷ ἀδελφῷ Δημητριανῷ
ἅμ[α] καὶ τῷ θείῳ Χρυσίππῳ
12 ἔστησαν τόδε σῆμα
μνήμης χάριν
θ(ανοῦσιν ?).

12. σῆμα was a very common general term for "tomb" used throughout Anatolia, especially in metrical epitaphs. More narrowly, the term referred to the tumulus or mound which marked the site of a burial. See Kubinska, *Les Monuments*, 23.

14. θ. This letter is not certain. There is a circular shape (of unclear significance) on the stone below the letters of l.13.

---

[3]The monument may have been dedicated before C.E. 250. The name Aurelia, borne by the primary dedicant and her deceased mother, suggests a date later than C.E. 212; but the style of the lettering resembles that of the mid-late second century, according to F.K. Dörner, "Bericht über eine Reise in Bithynien," *Österreichische Akademie der Wissenschaften, Phil.-Hist. Denkschriften* 75.1 (1959) 59–60.

(3.1) Limestone column from Bolu/Bithynion-Klaudiopolis.

> For the two purest ones
> who also had faith in God:[4]
> Markos Demetrianos, who served
> as first archon and general administrator
> and as agonothete[5] with honor,
> and (our) dearest mother, Aurelia
> Pannychas, we, Aurelia Demetriana,
> their daughter, and their son-in-law,
> Domitios Heliodoros, together with
> (her) brother Demetrianos and (her)
> uncle Chrysippos constructed this
> tomb in memory
> for the dead.

Publication: F. Becker-Bertau, *Die Inschriften von Klaudiupolis* (Bonn, 1986) 53–54, no. 44; F.K. Dörner, "Bericht über eine Reise in Bithynien," *Österreichische Akademie der Wissenschaften, Phil.-Hist. Denkschriften* 75.1 (1952) 59, no. 159.

---

[4] Reference to a singular God would be expected of Christians, but the more significant element for identifying this as a Christian monument is the word πιστεύσασιν. As used here to denote the relationship between the deceased and God, πιστεύειν carries a religious connotation which is peculiar to Christian usage. Cf. no. 3.5.

[5] The *agonothete* was the supervisor of games and public entertainments. Because of the very close relationship between public festivals and the imperial cult and/or traditional religion, the job is a surprising one in which to find a Christian. His service could have preceded his conversion, but see no. 3.4.

(3.2) Bomos (?) from Yakasimak/Eumeneia.

      [Αὐ]ρ(ήλιος) ᾿Αλέξανδ[ρος]
      [τ]οῦ ᾿Επιγόνου [Εὐ]–
      μενεὺς βουλε[υ]–
4   τῆς κατεσκεύα–
      σα τὸ ἡρῷον ἐ–
      μαυτῷ καὶ τῇ γυναικί μου Τατί[]–
      ῳ· εἰ δέ τις ἕτε–
8   ρος ἐμβάλῃ, ἔσ–
      ται αὐτῷ πρὸς τὸν Θεόν.

(3.2) Bomos (?) from Yakasimak/Eumeneia.[6]

> I, Aurelios Alexandros,
>
> son of Epigonos,
>
> a citizen of Eumeneia
>
> and member of the *boule*,
>
> constructed this shrine
>
> for myself and for my wife, Tation.
>
> If any other should inter
>
> (someone else), he will
>
> reckon with God.

Publication: Ramsay, *CB* 2, 519 f, no. 359.

---

[6] This monument likely dates from the mid-late third century. Cf. *MAMA* 4, nos. 355, 357 also from Eumeneia, dedicated by and/or for Aurelii, using the Eumeneian formula, and dated by Sullan era dates to C.E. 255 and 273 respectively; nos. 3.13 (Sebaste) and 3.18 (Apameia) following, and Jewish dedications nos. 1.19, 1.23. The same dating is probable for nos. 3.3, 3.4, 3.9 (Eumeneia), no. 3.6 (Sebaste), no. 3.8 (uncertain).

(3.3) Bomos from Ishikli/Eumeneia.

Αὐρ(ήλιος) Ζωτικὸς Πραξίου Εὐμενεὺς
βουλευτὴς κατεσκεύ–
ασεν τὸ ἡρῷον ἑαυτῷ
4 καὶ τεῖ γυναικί μου Γλυ–
κωνίδι καὶ τοῖς τέκνοις
μου Αὐρ(ηλίῳ) Ζωτικῷ τῷ υἱῷ
μου καὶ Διονυσίῳ καὶ
8 Ἀμμίᾳ τῇ θυγατρί μου
καὶ Μερτίνῃ τειθείδι· ἑτέρῳ
οὐδενὶ ἔξεστι τεθῆναι·
εἰ δέ τις ἐπιτηδεύσει ἕτε–
12 ρόν τινα θεῖναι, θήσει ἰς τὸ
ἱερώτατον ταμεῖον -x- βφ', τὸ δὲ
πάντων μεῖζον {ε} ἔσται αὐτῷ
πρὸς τὸν Θεόν.

2–3. κατεσκευασεν... ἑαυτῷ. The text shifts from 3rd person to 1st at line 4: γυναικί μου.

7. Διονυσίῳ. The status of Dionysios is unclear. τῷ υἱῷ in l.6 may refer to him as well as to Aurelios Zotikos, but (as written) some distinction seems to have been made between the two. W.H. Buckler, W.M. Calder, and C.W.M. Cox, "Asia Minor, 1924, III.1: Monuments from Central Phrygia," *JRS* 16 (1926) 70, suggest that Dionysios may have been an adopted child.

8. τειθείδι = τηθείδι.

(3.3) Bomos from Ishikli/Eumeneia.

> I, Aurelios Zotikos, son of Praxios,
> a citizen of Eumeneia and
> member of the *boule*, constructed
> this shrine for myself and also for
> my wife, Glykonas, and for my children:
> Aurelios Zotikos, my son, and
> Dionysios and Ammia, my daughter,
> and for Mertina, (my ?) aunt.
> For no other is it possible
> to be interred (here). If anyone
> should try to inter another
> he will pay to the imperial fiscus
> 2500 denarii and, more important than that,
> he will reckon with God.

Publication: W.H. Buckler, W.M. Calder, and C.W.M. Cox, "Asia Minor, 1924, III.1: Monuments from Central Phrygia," *JRS* 16 (1926) 69–70, no. 194; Ramsay, *CB* 2, 525, no. 368.

(3.4) Bomos from Ishikli/Eumeneia.

Εὐμο<ι>ροῖς
Αὐρ(ήλιος) Εὐτύχης Ἑρμο[ῦ]
ἐπίκλην "Ελιξ Εὐ–
4 μενεὺς καὶ ἄλ<λ>ων πόλ[ε]–
ων πολείτης, φυλῆς
Ἀδριανίδος, βουλευ–
τὴς καὶ γερεός,
8 κατεσκεύασεν τὸ ἡρῷ–
ον ἑαυτῷ καὶ τῇ σεμν–
οτάτῃ καὶ προσφιλεσ–
τάτῃ γυναικί μου
12 Μαρκέλλῃ καὶ τοῖς
ἑαυτῶν τέκνοις·
εἴ τις δὲ ἕτερος ἐ–
πιχειρήσει θεῖναι
16 τινα, ἔσται αὐτῷ
πρὸς τὸν ζῶντα
Θεόν.

1. Εὐμο<ι>ροῖς. This salutation may itself be indicative of Christian origin. Ramsay, *CB* 2, 523, suggests that this formula corresponds to the later, Latin *Bonis Bene*, apparently used by Christians as a substitute for *Dis Manibus*. Cf. no. 3.14.

7. γερεός = γερούσιος.

11. μου = αὐτοῦ.

(3.4) Bomos from Ishikli/Eumeneia.[7]

> To the happy (dead).
>
> Aurelios Eutyches, son of Hermos,
>
> nicknamed Helix, a citizen of Eumeneia
>
> and other cities, of the Hadrianic Phyle,
>
> a member of the *boule* and of the *gerousia*,[8]
>
> constructed this shrine
>
> for himself and for his most revered
>
> and beloved wife, Markella,
>
> and for their children.
>
> If any other endeavors
>
> to inter someone (here),
>
> he will reckon with the Living God.

Publication: W.H. Buckler, W.M. Calder, and C.W.M. Cox, "Asia Minor, 1924, III.1: Monuments from Central Phrygia," *JRS* 16 (1926) 80, no. 204; Ramsay, *CB* 2, 522, no. 364.

---

[7] On the left side of the bomos are carved three agonistic crowns, i.e. pertaining to games honoring the emperor and imperial cult, labelled respectively with the names of three cities: Sebaste and Stektorian in Phrygia and Brundisium in Italy. The purpose of the dedicant's association with these agonistic festivals is revealed by two carved tools, which appear with the crowns and which Louis Robert has identified as strigiles, an implement used to scrape off oil and grime after exercise or competition. See Louis Robert, *Hellenica* 11–12 (Paris: Maisonneuve, 1960) 423–24. Eutyches Helix was apparently a champion athlete, perhaps a wrestler to judge from his nickname. This explains the multiple citizenships alluded to in lines 4–5. Gifts of honorary citizenship to successful athletes were not unusual.

[8] The *gerousia* or Association of Elders, a common institution in the cities of Roman Anatolia, was apparently an elite social club, usually headquartered in a gymnasium (appropriately in this case). The *gerousia* seems not to have had any constitutional power, but probably exerted a certain influence due to the combined prestige of the membership.

(3.5) Sarcophagus from Ladik/Laodikea Katakekaumene.

M(ᾶρκος) Ἰού(λιος) Εὐ[γέ]νιος Κυρίλλου Κέλερος
Κουησσέως βουλ(ευτοῦ) / στρατευσ[ά]μενος ἐν τῇ
κατὰ Πισιδίαν ἡγεμονικῇ τάξι / καὶ γήμα[ς] θυγατέρα
4 Γαίου Νεστοριανοῦ συνκλητικοῦ / Φλ(αουίαν)
Ἰ[ο]υλ(ίαν) Φ[λ]αουιανὴν καὶ μετ' ἐπιτει[μ]ίας
στρατευσάμενον / ἐν δὲ τῷ μεταξὺ χρόνῳ κελεύσεως
[φ]οιτησάσης ἐπὶ Μαξιμίνου / τοὺς Χρ[ε]ιστιανοὺς
8 θύειν καὶ μὴ ἀπα[λ]λάσσεσθαι τῆς / στρατείας
πλείστας δὲ ὅσας βασάνου[ς] ὑπομείνας / ἐπὶ
Διογένους ἡγεμόνος σπουδάσας [τ]ε ἀπαλλαγῆναι /
τῆς
στρατείας τὴν τῶν Χρειστιανῶν πίστιν φυλάσσων /
12 χρόνον [ε] βραχὺν διατρείψας ἐν τῇ Λαοδικέων
πόλι / καὶ βουλήσει τοῦ παντοκράτορος Θεοῦ
ἐπίσκοπος / κατασταθ[εὶ]ς καὶ εἴκοσι πέντε ὅλοις ἔτεσιν
τὴν ἐπισκοπὴν / μετὰ πολ[λ]ῆς ἐπιτειμίας διοι[κ]ήσας
16 καὶ πᾶσαν τὴν ἐκλησίαν / ἀνοικοδο[μ]ήσας ἀπὸ

2. βουλ(ευτοῦ). This mention of *boule* membership seems to be directed towards the father of the dedicant, but the honor was hereditary. W.M. Calder, "Studies in Early Christian Epigraphy," *JRS* 10 (1920) 45, assumes that Kouessos was a village of Laodikea Katakekaumene and that the *boule* referred to was that of Laodikea.

3. ἡγεμονικῇ τάξι = *officium*. See Mason, *Greek Terms for Roman Institutions*, 92. Cf. no. 3.9, 1.9–10: ὀφικ[ί]ου.

4. συνκλητικοῦ (συγκλητικοῦ) = Roman senatorial rank. See Mason, *Greek Terms for Roman Institutions*, 88.

(3.5) Sarcophagus from Ladik/Laodikea Katakekaumene.[9]

I, Markos Ioulios Eugenios, son of Kyrillos Keler, (my father having been) a citizen of Kouessos and a member of the *boule*, (myself) having served as a soldier in the *officium* of the governor in (the province of) Pisidia and having married Flaouia Ioulia Flaouiane, daughter of Gaios Nestorianos, a Roman senator; and when, after having served with honor, subsequently, during the reign of (the emperor) Maximinos (Daia), an order was circulating for Christians to offer sacrifice (to the state gods) and not to be discharged from military service, having endured all possible tests by Diogenes, the governor (of Pisidia),[10] and having endeavored to be released from military service, guarding the faith of the Christians; and having spent a short time in the city of Laodikea (Katakekaumene), and by the will of Almighty God being ordained bishop, and having served as bishop with great distinction for twenty-five complete years; and having rebuilt the entire church from the foundations, together with all the embellishments accorded

---

[9] The monument probably was dedicated about C.E. 340, roughly twenty-five years after the events discussed in note no. 10 following.

[10] This persecution probably occurred about C.E. 311. Maximinos Daia held imperial office 305–313. The governor of Pisidia, Valerios Diogenes, is known from other inscriptions and was active ca. 311.

θεμελίων καὶ σύνπαντα τὸν περὶ αὐτὴν / κόσμον
τοῦτ᾽ ἐστιν στοῶν τε καὶ τ[ετ]ραστόων καὶ /
ζωγραφιᾶ[ν] καὶ κεντήσεων κὲ ὑδρείου καὶ
20 προπύλου καὶ πᾶσι τοῖς / λιθοξοικοῖς ἔργοις καὶ
πᾶ[σι ἁπ]αξαπλῶς κατασκευά[σας λειψόμε]νος τε
τὸν τῶν ἀνθρώπων / βίον ἐποίησα ἐμαυτῷ πέ[λτα τ]ε
καὶ σορὸν ἐν ᾗ τὰ προ[γεγραμμένα] ταῦτα ἐποίησα
24 ἐπιγρ<α>φῖνε / [εἰς κό]σμον τῆς τε ἐκ[λησίας κ]ὲ
τοῦ γένους μου.

23. πέλτα apparently refers to some sort of base upon which the
sarcophagus rested. See Kubinska, *Les Monuments*, 156ff.

it, including stoas, tetrastoas, paintings, mosaics, a fountain and vestibule, and all the ornamental stone work, and having constructed more-or-less everything, being about to leave (?) the world of men,[11] I prepared for myself this *pelta* and sarcophagus, on which I had these things engraved for public notice to honor the Church and my family.[12]

Publication: *MAMA* 1, no. 170; W.M. Calder, "Studies in Early Christian Epigraphy," *JRS* 10 (1920) 42ff.; W.M. Ramsay, "The Church of Lycaonia in the Fourth Century," in *Luke the Physician and Other Studies in the History of Religion* (London: Hodder and Stoughton, 1908) 339ff.

---

[11] W.M.Ramsay understood this to mean that the dedicant was preparing to become a hermit; see "The Church of Lycaonia in the Fourth Century," in *Luke the Physician and Other Studies in the History of Religion* (London: Hodder and Stoughton, 1908) 341. Calder, "Studies in Early Christian Epigraphy," *JRS* 10 (1920) 51ff, seems inclined to agree, but surely this interpretation is less likely than the obvious meaning presented by the need for a sarcophagus.

[12] The dedicant's obvious pride in his career and in his family, which presumably included his own children, and his great concern to describe fully the limits of his personal patronage are interesting characteristics to observe in a Christian bishop. He does not sound much like a potential hermit.

(3.6) Bomos (?) from Sivasli/Sebaste.

Αὐρ(ήλιος) Μεσσάλας β' Σεβασ-
τηνός, ἰατρός, βουλευτή[ς]
ζῶν ἑαυτῷ κατεσκεύα-
4 σεν καὶ τῇ συμβίῳ 'Αμμία
καὶ τῷ ἐκγόνῳ Μεσσάλᾳ
τὸ ἡρῷον· οὐκ ἔχοντος
ἐξουσίαν ἑτέρου ἐπισε-
8 νενκεῖν μετὰ τὴν τελευ-
τὴν τοῦ Μεσσάλα. εἰ δὲ μ[ή]
ἔσται αὐτῷ πρὸς τὸν
Θεόν.

(3.6) Bomos (?) from Sivasli/Sebaste.

> Aurelios Messalas the Younger,
> a citizen of Sebaste, a physician (and)
> member of the *boule*, constructed this
> shrine for himself, for (his) wife,
> Ammia, and for (his) son, Messalas.
> No one has authority to bury
> another after the death of Messalas.
> If (this rule) is not (obeyed),
> (the violator) will reckon with God.

Publication: Ramsay, *CB* 2, 560, no. 451.

(3.7) Stele from Ladik/Laodikea Katakekaumene.

> Αἴλ(ιος) Εὐ]γέ[νιος]
> Οὐαλερίνου βουλ(ευτής)
> ἀνέστησα τὸν τί–
> 4 τλον ζῶν τῇ γλυ–
> κυτάτῃ μου συνβίου
> Φλαβ(ία) Σωσάννῃ καὶ τῇ
> θρεπτῇ ἡμῶν Σωφρο–
> 8 νίῃ μνήμης χάριν· εἴ τις ἕ–
> τερον ἐπιβαλῖ δώσι λόγον Θεῷ.

3–4. τίτλον (τίτλος), referring to a funerary monument, appears to have been a fourth-century and later, usually Christian usage.

7. θρεπτῇ. This term is used often to refer to slaves bred in the household, but also can refer to adopted foundlings, which is the sense of the present translation. See Pliny the Younger, *Ep.* 10.65, concerning the status and support of *quos vocant* θρεπτούς.

(3.7) Stele from Ladik/Laodikea Katakekaumene.[13]

> I, Ailios Eugenios, son of
> Oualerinos (and) a member of the *boule*,
> set up this *titlos*, while
> still living, for my dearest
> wife, Flabia Sosanna, and
> our foster-daughter, Sophronia,
> in memory. If anyone should
> insert another (here), he will
> give account to God.

Publication: *MAMA* 1, no. 163.

---

[13] The monument likely dates from the second half of the fourth century. Reference to the monument/tomb as a *"titlos"* is compatible with such a date, and the name Flaouios (or Flabios) = Flavius/Flavia, the family name of Constantine (among others as shown by no. 3.6), became more widely popular in Anatolia during the reigns of Constantine and his sons. Cf. nos. 3.12, 3.16, and also no. 3.10, which may antedate Constantine.

(3.8) Bomos from Denizli Museum (provenance unknown).

Αὐρ(ηλίου) Χαριδή–
μου φιλοκυ–
νήγου ἑαυ–
4 τῷ καὶ τῇ γυ–
ναικὶ αὐτοῦ
Εὐκαρπίῃ κα[λ]ῇ
καὶ τέκνοις πεδίοι[ς]
8 αὐτοῦ. εἴ τις δὲ ἕτερος ἐπι[τη]–
δεύσει, ἔσται αὐτῷ πρὸς
τὸν Θεόν.

2–3. φιλοκυνήγου. In the Roman period, κυνηγέσιον / κυνήγιον referred not only to hunting, but also to wild animal fights in the arena. See, for example, the *Martyrdom of Polycarp* 12.2. This latter meaning cannot be ruled out here. Sheppard, ("Jews, Christians, and Heretics," 180) compares this epitaph to that of Eutyches Helix (no. 3.4) on the basis of the dedicants' "relaxed attitude to the traditional pursuits of the Greek gentleman."

(3.8) Bomos from Denizli Museum (provenance unknown).

> (The tomb) of Aurelios Charidemos,
> a lover of hunting,
> (which he prepared) for himself,
> and for his wife, fair Eukarpia,
> and for his natural-born children.
> If any other should try
> (to inter another),
> he will reckon with God.

Publication: Sheppard, "Jews, Christians, and Heretics," 180.

(3.9) Bomos (?) from Dede Keui/Eumeneia.

>   Αὐρ(ήλιος) Νεικέρως β' κατεσ–
>   κεύασεν τὸ ἡρῷον
>   [ἑ]αυτῷ καὶ γυναικ‹ὶ κ›αὶ
> 4   τέκνοις· ἔθηκα δὲ
>   φίλον. ἐνθάδε
>   κεκήδευτε Αὐρ(ήλιος)
>   Μάννος στρατιώτης
> 8   ἱππεὺς σαγιττάρις
>   δρακωνάρις ἐξ ὀφικ[ί]–
>   ου τοῦ λαμπροτάτου
>   ἡγεμόνος Καστρίο[υ]
> 12   Κώνσταντος.
>   ὃς δ' ἂν ἐπιτηδεύ–
>   σει ἕτερος, ἔστε αὐ–
>   [τῷ πρὸς τὸν Θεόν].

4. ἔθηκα. Note the momentary switch to a 1st person verb.

10. λαμπροτάτου = *clarissimus* (i.e. consular rank). See Mason, *Greek Terms for Roman Institutions*, 65.

15. [πρὸς τὸν Θεόν]. The restotation of the formula is virtually certain. No other common formula would fit the available space.

(3.9) Bomos (?) from Dede Keui/Eumeneia.

> Aurelios Neikeros the Younger
> constructed this shrine for himself
> and for (his) wife and children.
> I also authorized a friend (to be included).[14]
> Here has been interred Aurelios Mannos,
> a soldier, a mounted archer,
> standard-bearer in the *officium* of
> the governor, Kastrios Konstans,
> *clarissimus*.[15] Whoever should try
> (to include) another, will reckon with God.

Publication: Louis Robert, *Noms indigènes dans l'Asie-mineure greco-romaine* (Bibliothèque Archéologique et Historique de l'Institut Français d'Archéologie d'Istanbul 13; Paris: Maisonneuve, 1963) 361ff; Ramsay, *CB* 2, 529, no. 373.

---

[14] The willingness exemplified here to allow a non-family member into the family tomb has been viewed conventionally as a clear expression of specifically Christian charity, despite the very different attitude expressed (as we have seen) in many Christian epitaphs. However, the bond between this dedicant and his friend could also have been military service. Cf. Georgi Mihailov, *Inscriptiones Graecae in Bulgaria repertae* (Serdica: Academia Litterarum Bulgarica, Institutum Archaeologicum, Series Epigraphica, 2d. ed. 1970) 3.1, no. 1007; a monument from Philippopolos in Thrace, which seems likely also to commemorate Christians (the tomb is styled a *koimeterion*) and also in which a friend who was a military veteran was included among the family. Note also that the names of the wife and children in no. 3.9 are not cited.

[15] Aurelios Mannos presumably died while still on active duty at or near-by Eumeneia ca. C.E. 300. At about that time, one L. Kastrios Konstans (of consular rank) was governor of the province Phrygia-Caria.

99

(3.10) Stele from Iznik/Nikaea (? according to the copy of Ibrahim Efendi).

Φλ(άουιος) Ἰταλᾶς ἀπὸ προ-
τηκτόρων κατεσκεύ-
ασα τὸ κοιμητήριον ἐμαυτῷ
4 καὶ τῇ σεμνοτάτῃ μου συμβίῳ {μου} Αὐρηλίᾳ Ῥωμύλῃ
καὶ τῷ υἱῷ μου Αὐρηλίῳ Ῥωμύλ[ῳ]
καὶ τῇ κηδεστρίᾳ μου Αὐρηλίᾳ
8 Οὔρσῃ καὶ τῷ γυναικαδέλφῳ
μου Αὐρ(ηλίῳ) Σενεκιανῷ ἐπὶ τῷ
μετὰ τὸ κατατεθῆναι ἡμᾶς
ἀμφοτέρους τις ἂν σκύλῃ τὸ
12 κοιμητήριον, δώσει λόγον Θεῷ.

(3.10) Stele from Iznik/Nikaea (? according to the copy of Ibrahim Efendi).[16]

> I, Flaouios Italas, of the *protectores*,[17]
>
> constructed this *koimeterion* for myself,
>
> my most revered wife, Aurelia Romula,
>
> my son, Aurelios Romulos,
>
> my mother-in-law, Aurelia Oursa, and
>
> for my brother-in-law, Aurelios Senekianos,
>
> on the condition that after
>
> we are interred together,
>
> whoever should violate the *koimeterion*
>
> will give account to God.

Publication: Şahin, *Iznik* 1, no. 557; A.M. Schneider, "Die Römischen und Byzantinischen Denkmäler von Iznik-Nicaea," *Istanbuler Forschungen* 16 (1943) no.59.

---

[16] The monument may date from as early as the late third century. The possible Italian origin of the dedicant suggested by his name could indicate that the name Flaouios = Flavius may here have nothing to do with the dynasty of Constantine. The term *koimeterion* was already in use by then. Cf. 2.20, 3.15.

[17] The *protectores* were an elite corps of imperial bodyguards formed at least by the reign of Diocletian (284–305). Several other citations of the unit occur in Bithynia and especially at Nikomedia. See *TAM* 4.1, nos. 118, 137, 275, 383.

(3.11) Marble block from Konya/Ikonion.

[——————]μος Αὐρ(ήλιος) Μεῖρος υἱοὶ αὐτῷ
[ζῶντ]ες ἐπιτελέσαντες τῆς μνήμης χάριν.

[——]ος Τιηος ὁπλο–
4 [ποιὸ]ς καὶ Αὐρίλα Μα–
[μα?] ἡ γυνὴ αὐτοῦ
[ἀνέ]στησαν ἑαυτοῖς
[ζῶν]τες μνήμης
8 [χάρι]ν· ὃς δὲ ἂν
[ἕτερ]ον ἐπενβάλῃ
[δώσ]ει λόγον
[τῷ] Θεῷ.

(3.11) Marble block from Konya/Ikonion.

[_____ and] Aurelios Meiros, his sons,

while still living, finished this, in memory.

[___] Tieos, an armorer,

and Aurila Mama (?), his wife,

while still living, set up

(this) for themselves, in memory.

Whoever should insert another (here)

will give account to God.

Publication: W.H. Buckler, W.M. Calder, and C.W.M. Cox, "Asia Minor, 1924. Monuments from Iconium, Lycaonia, and Isauria," *JRS* 14 (1924) 34–35, no. 17.

(3.12) Stele from Ladik/Laodikea Katakekaumene.

✝

Φλα(ουία) Διογε-
νία ἀνέστησα
τὸν τίτλον
4 τοῦτον τῷ γλυ-
κυτάτῳ υείῷ
μου Σανβατίῳ
νουμέρου λαν-
8 κιαρίων ἰνιώρα[ν]
μνήμης χάριν·
εἰ δέ τις ἐξωτι]-
κὸν βαλῖ δώσι λ[ό]-
12 γον Θεῷ.

(3.13) Marble base from Seljukler/Sebaste.

[’Α]ντ(ώνιος) Πολλίων
παντοπώλης
αὐτῷ καὶ τῇ γυναι-
4 κὶ Αὐρ(ηλίᾳ) ’Αμμίᾳ Ζην-
οδότου καὶ τοῖς τέ-
κνοις αὐτοῦ κατεσ-
κεύασεν τὸ ἡρ-
8 ῷον· εἰ δέ τις ἕτερον
ἐπισενένκῃ τινά ἔσ-
τε αὐτῷ πρὸς τὸν Θεόν.
ἔτους τμ', μη(νὸς) θ', κ'.

(3.12) Stele from Ladik/Laodikea Katakekaumene.

+

> I, Flaouia Diogenia,
> set up this *titlos*
> for my dearest son,
> Sanbatios, of the
> *numerus lanciariorum*
> *iuniorum*,[18] in memory.
> If anyone should cast it
> out (from its place),
> he will give account to God.

Publication: *MAMA* 1, no. 167.

(3.13) Marble base from Seljukler/Sebaste.

> Antonios (?) Pollion,
> a dealer in general merchandise,
> constructed this shrine for himself and for his wife
> Aurelia Ammia, daughter of Zenodotos,
> and for his children.
> If anyone should insert another,
> he will reckon with God.
> (Dedicated in the) year 340
> (Sullan era = C.E. 255/56), month 8, (day) 20.

Publication: Ramsay, *CB* 2, 560, no. 449.

---

[18] This is a unit of spearmen.

(3.14) Stele from Izmit/Nikomedia.

Εὐμοίριος
Πάπος
'Αράδιος ξυλο–
4 γλύφος κῖμε
λείψανον ἐν–
θάδε πρόμοι–
ρος κακῶν ἐτῶν
8 + μα'. χαίρετε
παροδῖτε.

1. Εὐμοίριος. As written, this must be a name, but cf. the salutation in no. 3.4.

(3.15) Stele from Iznik/Nikaea (?).

+
Αὐρήλιος Χρῆσ–
τος οἰκῶν ἐν
τετραπύλω, λι–
4 θίνῳ, τὴν τέ–
χνην ἀρτοπώ–
λης, ἐκτησάμ–
ην τὸ κυμητήριο–
8 ν σὺν τῇ γυνεκὶ
μου Κ<α>λημέρα
καὶ τοῖς τέκνοις.

7-8. κυμητήριον = κυμητήριον. This alternate spelling appears fairly often.

(3.14) Stele from Izmit/Nikomedia.[19]

> Eumoirios Papos,
> a citizen of Arados (in Phoenicia),
> a wood carver,
> lies here before his time, a
> ✝ remnant of 41 unlucky years.
> Farewell passerby.

Publication: Louis Robert, "Documents d'Asie mineure," *BCH* 102 (1978) 413ff.

(3.15) Stele from Iznik/Nikaea (?).[20]

> I, Aurelios Chrestos,
> living in Four Stone Gates
> (in Nikaea ?), a baker
> by trade, acquired
> this *koimeterion*, together
> with my wife, Kalemera,
> and (our) children.

Publication: Şahin, *Iznik* 1, no. 553.

---

[19] Louis Robert, "Documents d'Asie mineure," *BCH* 102 (1978) 414, dates the monument to the late third century on the basis of the "discrete" cross, but a fourth century date is equally likely.

[20] The monument is probably post-Constantinian, perhaps from the mid-late fourth century. Cf. no. 3.17, which is similar in the formulation of the epitaph and which carries a chi-rho emblem.

(3.16) Limestone column from Ladik/Laodikea Katakekaumene.

+

Αὐρ<η>λ(ία) Θε–
σεβὶς ἀνεσ–
τησα Φλα(βίῳ)
4 Νικίᾳ τῷ ἀν–
δρί μου καὶ
αὐραρίῳ +
μνήμης
8 χάριν.

(3.17) "Grave House" from Iznik/Nikaea.

ΑΥΡΣΠΟΥΔΑΣΙΣΝΙΚΕΕΥ
ΟΙΚΩΝΕΝ   ΦΥΛΗΑΥΡΗ
ΖΩΝΕΜΑΥ ⳨ ΛΙΑΝΗ
ΤΩΚΑ ΚΗΠΟΥΡΟΣ ΤΕΣΚΕΥ
ΚΑΙΤΗΣΕΜΝΟ   ΑΣΑ
ΤΑΤΗΜΟΥΣΥΒΙΩΑΥΡΘΕΟΔ

1   Αὐρ(ήλιος) Σπούδασις Νικεεὺ[ς]
(4)   κηπουρὸς
2-3   οἰκῶν ἐν φυλῇ Αὐρη–/ λιανῇ
3–4–5 ζῶν ἐμαυ–/ τῷ κα–τεσκεύ–/ ασα
5   καὶ τῇ σεμνο–
6   τάτῃ μου συ<μ>βίῳ Αὐρ(ηλίᾳ) Θεοδ[ώρᾳ].

(3.16) Limestone column from Ladik/Laodikea Katakekaumene.

+

> I, Aurelia Thesebis,
> set up (this monument)
> for my husband, **+**
> Flabios Nikias, a goldsmith,
> in memory.

Publication: *MAMA* 1, no. 214.

(3.17) "Grave House" from Iznik/Nikaea.

☧

> I, Aurelios Spoudasis, a citizen of
> Nikaea, an orchard keeper,
> living in the Phyle Aureliana,
> while still living, constructed (this)
> for myself and for my
> most revered wife, Aurelia Theodora.

Publication: Şahin, *Iznik* 1, no. 554.

(3.18) Bomos (?) from Dineir (?)/Apameia.

῎Ετους τμγ', μ(ηνὸς) θ', κ'. Αὐρ(ήλιος) ᾽Αρτέμ[ας]
ἐποίησα τὸ ἡρῷον ἐμαυτῷ [καὶ τῇ γυναικί]
μου Τατίᾳ κὲ τοῖς τέκνοῖς μ[ου· εἰς ὃ ἕτερος]
4 οὐ τεθήσεται· εἰ δέ τις ἐπι[τηδεύσει ἔσ]–
ται αὐτῷ πρὸς τὸν ἀθάνα[τον Θεόν].

(3.18) Bomos (?) from Dinar (?)/Apameia.

> In the year 343 (Sullan era = C.E. 258/59),
> month 9, (day) 20, I, Aurelios Artemas,
> built this shrine for myself, for my
> wife, Tatia, and for my children.
> No other is to be put in (here).
> If anyone tries (to inter another),
> he will reckon with the Deathless God.[21]

Publication: Ramsay, *CB* 2, 534, no. 388.

---

[21] The epithet "Deathless God" has been described by A.R.R. Sheppard, "Jews, Christians, and Heretics in Acmonia and Eumeneia," *AS* 29 (1979) 175, as " almost certainly Jewish," but cf. no. 4.16, 1.24.

CHAPTER 4

THE EPITAPHS AND EARLY-CHRISTIAN RELIGION

The Anatolian funerary monuments/epitaphs provide some information also about the religious beliefs of the Christians who produced them. This information (not surprisingly) is limited both in volume and in detail. After all, the scarcity of explicit religious data in the Anatolian epitaphs (Christian and non-Christian alike) has been noted already. (pp. 6, 39) In addition, our ability to understand even the few data available in the epitaphs is inhibited by a number of problems/issues.

For example, precise attribution of particular beliefs rarely is possible because of the difficulty (alluded to earlier, pp. 3-4) of distinquishing the separate influences of the purchaser/dedicant, of the deceased (if different), and of the professional stoneworker on the final form of the monument/epitaph. Furthermore, regardless of whether we attribute specific data to Christian stoneworkers or to their Christian customers, the epitaphs express the sentiments of a somewhat different segment of the Christian population than we encounter generally in Christian literature. Those responsible for the creation of the epitaphs were, for the most part, ordinary, "non-professional" Christians. They may not have been entirely "average" in a social or economic sense (pp. 77-78), but probably the large majority (even if they happened to be literate) never would have authored a formal religious text. Indeed, the issue of literacy aside, most may not have been familiar with even such basic texts as the New Testament documents. The epitaphs, at least, contain very few allusions to or quotations from New Testament authors/texts. (nos. 2.15, 4.1; and p. 43, pertaining to the formula: δώσει λόγον τῷ Θεῷ)

Interestingly enough, the word "Christian" itself is misspelled in most of the epitaphs which explicitly reference the religious affiliation of Christian dead. The most common rendering of "Christian" spelled the word with η rather than ι (i.e. Χρηστιανός: nos. 2.4, 2.5, 2.7, 2.11), while others used the diphthong ει (i.e., Χρειστιανός: nos. 2.1, 2.2, 2.3, 2.6, 2.19?, 3.5). This circumstance could be (and has been) interpreted simply as a linguistic/ phonological phenomenon without additional intellectual or theological significance. That is to say, one could assume that the variant spellings all really were intended to render a word meaning "followers of the anointed", and that some orthographical confusion may have occurred due (probably) to the general merging of the sounds of ι, η, ε, and ει in spoken koine. The epitaphs in this collection have offered numerous examples of such vowel confusion, and the same phenomenon is evident in papyrological texts as well. However, many of the epitaphs which contain these apparent "misspellings" (and especially those using the form Χρηστιανός) provide no examples of similar confusion in the spelling of other words, and, thereby, force us to consider the possibility that some at least of the misspellings may stem from conscious religious perceptions rather than from linguistic confusion. One is reminded of Tertullian's complaint in *Apol.* 3.5: "In truth, '*Christianus*,' as far as definition is concerned, is derived from (the word) 'anointing;' but, on the other hand, when you pronounce it incorrectly, '*Chrestianus,*' (for you have an inaccurate understanding of the name) it is concocted from the word for 'sweetness' or 'kindness.'[1] Presumably, Tertullian was addressing non-Christians, whose confusion of χριστός and χρηστός easily could stem from a lack of familiarity with Judaic messiah doctrine, but the possible presence of the same "mistake" in the Christian epitaphs is rather more curious.[2]

In light of the preceding characteristic in particular, we must wonder to what degree these ordinary Christians of Anatolia conformed to any of the sets of beliefs and/or practices sponsored by Christian intellectuals through the literary medium.[3] Scholars have tended to assume that the epitaphs should reflect exactly the landscape of Christian literature, but certain religious matters, which appear from the literary perspective to have dominated early-Christian thought and life, scarcely are noticeable in the epitaphs, and sometimes seem flatly to be

---

[1] *Christianus vero, quantum interpretatio est, de unctione deducitur. Sed et cum perperam Chrestianus pronuntiatur a vobis (nam nec nominis certa est notitia penes vos), de suavitate vel benignitate compositum est.* For a similar complaint, see also Lactantius, *De Div. Instit.* 4.7.

[2] M.J. Edwards. "Χρηστός in a Magical Papyrus," *Zeitschrift für Papyrologie und Epigraphik* 85 (1991) 232–36, suggests that some gnostics purposefully may have substituted Χρηστός for Χριστός, but even more radical explanations of the phenomenon are possible.

[3] The well-known statement of Gregory of Nyssa (*De Deitate Filii et Spiritus Sancti, PG* 46, 557) concerning the theological awareness of average Christians may be misleading: "If you ask for your change, someone philosophizes to you on the Begotten and the Unbegotten. If you ask the price of bread, you are told: 'The Father is greater and the Son inferior.' If you ask, 'Is the bath ready?' someone answers, 'The Son was created from nothing.'" The translation is quoted from Timothy E. Gregory, *Vox Populi* (Columbus, OH: Ohio State University Press, 1979) 3.

contradicted. This circumstance may result (in part) simply from the specialized focus of the funerary medium, but may also reflect genuine differences between the beliefs, practices, and lives of different sorts of Christians.

The epitaphs seldom refer to persecution (no. 3.5) and/or martyrdom. (no. 4.2, 4.3, 4.4, 4.7) Instead, as we have seen, they show us Christians who identified their religious affiliation explicitly in their epitaphs (nos. 2.1, 2.2, 2.3, 2.4, 2.5, 2.6, 2.7, 2.11, 2.18, 2.19, 3.5); who expected city and imperial officials to collect fines from anyone who should dare to violate their tombs (nos. 2.15, 2.20); who held public offices (nos. 3.1, 3.2, 3.3, 3.4, 3.6, 3.7), served in the army (nos. 3.10, 3.11, 3.12, 4.4, 4.11), and participated in athletic games. (no. 3.4) Such Christians do not reveal the sort of estrangement from conventional society that usually is associated with persecution.

Because (no doubt) epitaphs tended to be family memorials, often commissioned by still-living individuals to honor themselves and other family members, they rarely honor sexual abstention or other ascetic practices which run counter to normal family existence. (nos. 4.5, 4.6) In fact, to judge only from the repeated warnings about intrusion into family tombs, family identity appears to have been at least as strong as any Christian group identity.

The epitaphs preserve only faint traces of the doctrinal divisions and controversies of the third-fourth centuries. (nos. 4.7, 4.8, 4.9, 4.10, 4.11) The epitaphs from these same centuries (during which the nature of Jesus/Christ was under heavy debate) virtually never mention "Jesus" or "Christ" apart from the title "Christian." Nos. 2.13 and 2.15 acknowledge "the Holy Shepherd," but most theological references are to Θεός / "God." "God" is, for example, the normal guarantor of the privacy of Christian tombs. Jesus/Christ almost never appears as guardian of the tomb, although, in at least one notable case, the job could go to the «ἄγγελος» of (apparently) a local holy-man. (nos. 4.12, 4.13) Jesus/Christ as an entity distinct from Θεός may not even have been regarded by all of these "Christians" as a necessary factor in individual "salvation" — a concept which itself, of course, could have been variously interpreted. (nos. 4.14, 4.15, 4.16) This absence of Jesus/Christ also is especially provocative in light of the misspelling of "Christian" discussed above.

A number of the epitaphs refer to "Judgment" and/or "Judgment Day," usually within the context of one of the warnings about the consequences of violating the tomb. (nos. 2.20, 4.17, 4.18) Within this context, however, "Judgment" appears to be something which happens to others, i.e. the violators, and which could be called down upon the violators through the expression of a curse. This sort of summoning of the divine power puts real control into the hands of the conjurer/dedicant, and certainly does not express immediate concern with any Judgment which might await the dedicant him/herself. The use of curse formulae, therefore, even if phrased in Christianized language, may reflect more than a merely superficial continuation of traditional attitudes towards death, burial, and the divine. Unfortunately, we have no data regarding the narrow specifics of body placement, grave goods, etc., which might help to clarify the issue, but a small number of later epitaphs, which use familiar curse formulae in a slightly different way, suggest that the notion of a personal judgement may only gradually have become a part of the average Anatolian Christian mentality. (no. 4.19)

The preceding examples clearly do not exhaust the supply of problems and questions pertaining to early-Christian religion which are raised by the epitaphs. In fact, all of the examples offered could be subsumed within larger, theoretical questions pertaining to the reality or nature of "popular religion." They do, however, offer a fair illustration of the range of work that needs to be done. Surprisingly few scholars ever have investigated the religious dimensions of the Christian epitaphs, and most of their pioneer commentaries are methodologically out-of-date. A new generation of scholarship now is required.

(4.1) Stele from Salamis (Attika).

+

> + Οἶκος αἰώνιος
> Ἀγάθωνος ἀνα-
> γνώ<στου> καὶ Εὐφημίας
> 4 ἐν δυσὶ θήκαις
> ἰδίᾳ ἑκάστῳ ἡμῶν·
> εἰ δέ τις τῶν ἰδίων <ἢ>
> ἕτερός τις τολ-
> 8 μήσῃ σῶμα κατα-
> θέσθαι ἐνταῦθα
> παρὲξ τῶν δύο
> ἡμῶν, λόγον δώ-
> 12 η τῷ Θεῷ καὶ ἀ-
> νάθεμα ἤτω
> μαράνα θάν.

12–14. ἀνάθεμα ἤτω μαράνα θάν may represent a quote from 1 Cor 16:22: εἰ τις οὐ φιλεῖ τὸν Κύριον, ἤτω ἀνάθεμα. Μαράνα θά; "If anyone does not love the Lord, let him be cursed. The Lord comes."

(4.1) Stele from Salamis (Attika).[4]

✝

✝ Eternal home[5]

of the reader, Agathon,

and Euphemia, in two vaults,

each one our private property.

If any other should dare

to inter a body

from their own family (?)

here beside our two,

he will give account to God

and be cursed.

The Lord comes.

Publication: *Corpus Inscriptionum Atticarum* 3.2, no. 3509 = *CIG*, no. 9303.

---

[4] Though not actually found in Anatolia, this epitaph has several characteristics in common with the Anatolian dedications.

[5] This description of the tomb is fairly common in the Anatolian epitaphs, and (especially given the architectural motifs often utilized in Anatolian funerary monuments) may reflect a traditional notion that the spirts of the dead do inhabit the tomb for eternity. See note no. 6 following. The terminology is less common in the Christian epitaphs, but does appear several times. Cf. similar language in no. 4.12. One must wonder if the Christian usage is anachronistic or purposeful.

(4.2) Marble reliquary from Şuhut/Synnada.

(A) ᾿Ὧδε ἔνα Τρο–
    φίμου τοῦ μ–
    άρτυρος ὀστε–
4   α.

(B) Τίς ἂν δὲ ταῦ–
    τα τὰ ὀστέα
    ἐκβάλῃ ποτὲ
8   ἔσται αὐτῷ
    πρὸς τ[ὸ(ν)] Θεό–
    ν.

(4.3) Limestone block from near Gudelisin/Derbe.

    Νοῦννο[ς]
    καὶ ᾿Ουαλέ–
    ριος ἐκόσ–
4   μησαν Παῦ–
    λον τὸν μάρ–
    τυραν,
    μ(νήμης) χ(άριν).

(4.2) Marble reliquary from Şuhut/Synnada.[6]

    (A) Here within (are) the bones of Trophimos, the martyr.[7]

    (B) Whoever, accordingly, should throw these bones out, will reckon with God.

Publication: G. Mendel, "Catalogue du Musée de Brousse," *BCH* 33 (1909) 342ff, no. 102.

(4.3) Limestone block from near Gudelisin/Derbe.[8]

    Nonnos and Oualerios

    (with this monument)

    honored Paulos, the martyr,[9]

    in memory.

Publication: W.M. Ramsay (ed.), *Studies in the History and Art of the Eastern Provinces of the Roman Empire* (Aberdeen University Studies 20; Aberdeen: Aberdeen University Press, 1906) 60–61, no.34.

---

[6] The reliquary is made in the shape of a house, a motif employed also in one type of Anatolian sarcophagus. A large number of Anatolian stelai also were carved to resemble the façade of a house. Cf. no. 2.2.

[7] The Trophimos commemorated here may be St. Trophimos of Antioch in Pisidia, martyred in the reign of the emperor Probus (276-282).

[8] The stone seems to represent a particular type of tombstone produced near this area, which was finished only on one side. However, rather than being a normal funerary monument, the stone may possibly have formed part of the wall of a martyrium or chapel.

[9] This Paulos is otherwise unknown.

(4.4) Stele from Izmit/Nikomedia.

Φλ(άουιος) Μαξιμῖνος σκουτά–
ριος σινάτωρ ἀνέστη–
σα τὴν στίλην τῷ υἱῷ
4 μου Ὀκτίμῳ ζήσαντι
ἔτη ε', ἡμέρας ιε'· τμηθὶς
ὑπὸ ἰατροῦ ἐμαρτύρη–
σεν. Fla(vius) Maximinus scu-
8 tarius sinator levavi sta-
tu(am) filio meo Octemo, vixit an-
nos V, dies XV; precisus a medico
(h)ic postus est ad martyres.

2. σινάτωρ (l.8. *sinator*) = *senator*.

(4.5) Stele from Kosmer/territory of Laodikea Katakekaumene.

[– – – – –πρεσ]–/ βύτερος ἀ[νέσ]–/ τησα τῆς ἀ–/
δελφὲς μου Α[ὐρ(ηλία)] / Ἀππεία κὲ Ναι[– –?] /
παρθένες, / μνήμης χά[ριν]· / ὃς δ' ἂν καταβ[άλ]η /
4 τὴν ἰστήλ[ην], / δώσει λόγο[ν τῷ] / Θεῷ.

3-4. τῆς ἀδελφὲς = ταῖς ἀδελφαῖς. Note *MAMA* 1, no. 164a = *MAMA* 7, no. 93, a monument also from the territory of Laodikea Katakekaumene and also dedicated by a presbyter for his "sister."

(4.4) Stele from Izmit/Nikomedia.

> I, Flaouios Maximinos, a member
> of the *scutarii*[10] and a *senator*,[11]
> set up this stele for my son, Oktimos,
> who lived five years and fifteen days.
> Maimed by (his) doctor/surgeon,
> he became a martyr.[12]

Publication: *TAM* 4.1, no. 367.

(4.5) Stele from Kosmer/territory of Laodikea Katakekaumene.

> [I,_____], a presbyter, set up (this stele) for my sisters,
> Aurelia Appeia and Nai[- - ?], virgins, in memory; whoever
> should throw over this stele will give account to God.

Publication: *MAMA* 7, no. 66.

---

[10] This dedication probably dates from no earlier than the mid-to-late fourth century. In that period, the *scutarii* were regiments in the *scholae*, (i.e. the imperial bodyguard) which were armed with a heavy shield = *scutum*. Flavios Maximinos also possibly could have been a shield-maker, the original meaning of *scutarius*.

[11] *Senator* was a senior, non-commissioned officer rank in the *scholae*.

[12] The allusion to martyrdom here is metaphorical and a product of a father's grief and anger. The epitaph has been included to highlight the scarcity of surviving dedications to more conventional Christian martyrs.

(4.6) Marble (?) block from Kadin Khan/Laodikea Katakekaumene.

(A) Γάειος Εἰούλιος
Πατρίκιος τῇ γλυ-
κυτάτῃ μου θίᾳ
4 'Ορεστίνῃ ἐνκρα-
τευσαμένῃ ἀν-
έστησα μνή-
μης χάριν.

(B) Γάειος Εἰούλιος
Πατρίκιος τῷ
ποθινοτάτῳ
μου ἀδελφῷ
12 Μνησιθέῳ ἀ-
νέστησα τὴν τίτλ[ον]
ταύτην μνήμης χάρι[ν].

4-5. ἐνκρατευσαμένῃ. W.M. Calder, "The Epigraphy of the Anatolian Heresies," in *Anatolian Studies Presented to Sir William Mitchell Ramsay* (Manchester: Manchester University Press, 1923) 87, suggests that this term represents the name of a formally-constituted, heretical sect of Encratites to which the members of this family belonged. Clearly, however, this supposition cannot be proven.

(4.6) Marble (?) block from Kadin Khan/Laodikea Katakekaumene.

> (A) I, Gaeios Eioulios Patrikios,
>> for my dearest
>> aunt, Orestina,
>> who lived in continence,
>> set up (this monument)
>> in memory.

> (B) I, Gaeios Eioulios Patrikios,
>> for my most fondly-remembered
>> brother, Mnesitheos,
>> set up this *titlos,*
>> in memory.

Publication: Calder, "The Epigraphy of the Anatolian Heresies," 87f, no. 9.

(4.7) Marble slab from Payamalani/Sebaste.

    [✝] 'Ενταῦθα κῖται
    [ὁ] ἅγιος Παυλῖνος
    [μο]ίστης κ<αὶ> κοινωνὸς
4 [ἔχω]ν τὴν χάριν
    [Θ(εο)ῦ] ἔτη πε'.
    ['Ο ἅγ]ιος Τρόφιμος
    [μά]ρτυς.

3 μοίστης = μύστης.

(4.7) Marble slab from Payamalani/Sebaste.

> \+ Here lies the holy man,
>
> Paulinos, *mystes*[13] and *koinonos*,[14]
>
> holding the grace of God
>
> for eighty-five years.
>
> The holy man, Trophimos,[15]
>
> martyr, (lies here too ?).

Publication: W.M. Calder, "Early-Christian Epitaphs from Phrygia," *AS* 5 (1955) 37–38, no. 7; William Tabbernee, "Montanist Regional Bishops: New Evidence from Ancient Inscriptions," *Journal of Early Christian Studies* 1.3 (1993) 269–72.

---

[13] William Tabbernee, "Montanist Regional Bishops: New Evidence from Ancient Inscriptions," *Journal of Early Christian Studies* 1.3 (1993) 271: "By the end of the fifth century C.E., *mystes* was used, in catholic circles, not merely in the sense of initiator into the 'divine mysteries,' but also as a synonym for metropolitan...In the Paulinos inscription, *mystes* serves not only as a parallel term to *koinonos* but...gives some added information about the function of the person so designated."

[14] This term probably confirms that the dedication honors a leader of the Montanist sect. Montanist *koinonoi* were regional bishops. However, Montanist dedications are not always so easy to identify. W.M. Calder (among others) in a series of articles argued that the "Christians for Christians" formula was exclusively a Montanist emblem. This view (for a time) won wide acceptance, but is now suspect.

[15] Calder, "Early Christian Epitaphs from Phrygia," *AS* 5 (1955) 37, suggests that this is the same Trophimos commemorated in no. 4.2, but such a coincidence seems unlikely.

(4.8) Marble (?) doorstone from Uşak/Akmonia (?).

Διογᾶς ἐβίσκο–
πος ᾽Αμμίῳ πρεσ–
βυτέρᾳ μνήμης
4   χάριν.

(4.9) Stele from Kadin Khan/Laodikea Katakekaumene.

☧

Λεύκιος ἀνέσ–
θησα τῷ γλυκυ–
τάτῳ μου πα–
4   τρὶ ᾽Αβρᾳ τῷ εὐ–
λαβεστάτῳ πρεσ–
βιθέρῳ θῆς τοῦ
Θεοῦ ἁγίας ἐ–
8   κλησίας τῶν
Ναυατῶν ἐν ᾗ
κὲ ἐπολιθεύ–
σατο {ἀνεσθη–
12   σα} μνήμης [χ]άριν.

1. ἀνέσθησα = ἀνέστησα. Note also θ = τ in line 5–6 (πρεσβιθέρῳ, θῆς) and line 10 (ἐπολιθεύσατο).

128

(4.8) Marble (?) doorstone from Uşak/Akmonia (?).

> Diogas, the bishop,
>
> (dedicated this monument)
>
> for Ammion, a (female)
>
> presbyter,[16]
>
> in memory.

Publication: Elsa Gibson, "Montanist Epitaphs at Usak," *Greek, Roman and Byzantine Studies* 16.4 (1975) 437; Marc Waelkens, *Die Kleinasiatischen Türsteine* (Mainz: Philipp von Zabern, 1986) 147, no. 367.

(4.9) Stele from Kadin Khan/Laodikea Katakekaumene.

$$ ⳨ $$

> I, Leukios, set
>
> up (this monument)
>
> for my dearest
>
> father, Abras,
>
> most pious presbyter
>
> of the holy
>
> Church of God of the
>
> Novatians, in which
>
> also he was a member,
>
> in memory.

---

[16] Apparent reference to a female presbyter perhaps marks this as a Montanist dedication also. The presence of women presbyters among the Montanists is noted by Epiphanius (*Panarion* 49.2).

(4.10) Stele (?) from Bash Hüyük/Laodikea Katakekaumene.

Αὐ(ρηλία) Οὐαλεντίλλη κὲ Λεόντιος κὲ Κατμαρος
ἀνεστήσαμεν / τὴν τίτλον ταύτην Εὐγενίῳ
πρ(εσβυτέρῳ) πολλὰ καμόντος ὑπὲρ / τῆς ἁγίας τοῦ
4   Θεοῦ ἐκλησίας τῶν Καθαρῶν ζῶντες μνήμης χάριν. /

Πρῶτο<ν> μὲν ὑμνήσω Θεὸν τὸν πάντει ὁρῶντα,
δεύτερον ὑμνήσω πρῶτον ἄγγελον ΟΣΤΙΣΑΙΤΡΣΙΝ

Εὐγενίου θανεόντος πολλὴ μνήμη ἐπὶ γέη·
8   Εὐγένιε, νέος θάνες· ἡελίοιο σε γὰρ ἐγίνωσκαν πάντες,
ἀντολίη τε δύσις τε με<σ>ινβρία τε κὲ ἄρκτος
ὄλβῳ τε πλούτῳ τε εὐγενίη τε κὲ θάρσι·
πένησιν ζῶν θάρσος, κώμῃ τ' ἔξοχος ἁπάντων·
12 σὲν Φρυγίη τ' Ἀσίη τε κὲ Ἀντολίη τε δύδιστο.

3–4. ἁγίας...Καθαρῶν. Calder, "Epigraphy of the Anatolian Heresies," 69, suggests that Cathari and Novatians were "of course" alternate names for a single sect, but this seems difficult to prove in the present context.

6. ΟΣΤΙΣΑΙΤΡΣΙΝ. Calder, "Epigraphy of the Anatolian Heresies," 78, offers two (very problematic) readings of these letters, both involving multiple "omitted" letters and both aimed at making TP(..) a reference to the Novatian Trinity, in which supposedly the πρῶτον ἄγγελον = the Son.

12. δύδιστο. Calder, "Epigraphy of the Anatolian Heresies," 80, suggests that this word is a pluperfect formed from δεύομαι or δίζημι "in the sense of ποθῶ."

(4.10) Stele (?) from Bash Hüyük/Laodikea Katakekaumene.

We, Aurelia Oualentille and Leontios and Katmaros, while still living, set up this *titlos* for Eugenios, the presbyter, who labored much for the sake of the holy Church of God of the Pure Ones, in memory.

First then, I will praise God who sees everywhere;
secondly, I will praise the First Angel ΟΣΤΙΣΑΙΤΡΣΙΝ.

Of dead Eugenios, (there is) much recollection upon the Earth.
You died young, Eugenios, yet everyone under the sun-
east and west and south and north-
knew you by (your) prosperity, wealth, nobility, and courage.
Living, (you provided ?) courage for the poor,
and, in the village, were preeminent in every way.
Phrygia, Asia, and the East mourn (?) for you.

Publication: Calder, "The Epigraphy of the Anatolian Heresies," 76ff, no. 4.

(4.11) Limestone block from Ladik/Laodikea Katakekaumene.

Φλα(ουία) Μαρία Σελεύ-
κισσα ἀνέστησα τῷ
ἀνδρί μου Παύλου
4 ἀπὸ καμπιδουκτό-
ρων ὠρδεναρίου
μνήμης χάριν καὶ
ἄν τις ἐπιχιρίσι ἔσ[τα]ι
8 πρὸς τὴν Τριάδαν.

(4.11) Limestone block from Ladik/Laodikea Katakekaumene.

> I, Flaouia Maria Seleukissa,
> set up (this monument)
> for my husband, Paulos,
> an *ordinarius*[17] of the *campidoctorum*,[18]
> in memory; and should
> anyone attempt to damage (it),
> he will reckon with the Trinity.

Publication: *MAMA* 1, no. 168.

---

[17] *Ordinarius* was a non-commissioned officers' rank.
[18] A *campidoctor* was a regimental drill instructor.

(4.12) Marble bomos from Emircik/Eumeneia.

[Οὐνόμασιν σεμνοῖσιν] / ἰσόψηφος δυσὶ τοῦτ[ο,] /
Γάιος, ὡς ἅγιος, ὡς ἀγ[α]– / θος προλέγω· /
ζωὸς ἐὼν τοῦτον τύμ– / βον τις ἔτευξεν ἑαυτῷ /
4 Μούσαις ἀσκηθεὶς / Γάιος πραγματικὸς /
ἠδ᾽ ἀλόχῳ φιλίῃ Τατίῃ / τέκεσίν τε ποθητοῖς /
ὄφρα τὸν ἀίδιον τοῦ– / τον ἔχωσι δόμον /
σὺν Ρουβῇ μεγάλοιο / Θ(εο)ῦ θεράποντι. /

8 [Ο]ὐκ ἔσχον πλοῦτον πολὺν / εἰς βίον, οὐ πολὺ χρῦμα, /
γράμμασι δ᾽ ἠσκήθην ἐκπο– / νέσας μετρίοις, /
ἐξ ὧν τοῖσι φίλοισιν ἐπή[ρ]– / κεον ὡς δύναμίς μοι, /
σπουδὴν ἣν εἶχ]ον πᾶσι / χαρίζομενος· /
12 τοῦτο γὰρ ἦν μοι τερπ[νὸν] / ἐπαρκεῖν, εἴ τις ἔχρηζε[ν], /
ὡς ἄλλων ὄλβος τέρψιν / ἄγει κραδίῃ. /

(4.12) Marble bomos from Emircik/Eumeneia.[19]

I, Gaios, whose name equals in numerical value two solemn words,
"agios" (holy) and "agathos" (good), proclaim this:[20]
A man, Gaios the lawyer, practised in the arts, while still alive,
built this tomb for himself
and for (his) dear wife Tatia, and (their) lamented children
in order that they might have this eternal home
with Roubes, servant of the Great God.[21]

I did not have great wealth in life, nor many possessions;
but I worked hard (and) acquired a fair amount of intellectual skills,
through which I helped (my) friends as much as possible—
being eager, indeed, to oblige them all.
For that matter, it pleased me to help if anyone was in need;
just as for others wealth gladdens the heart.

---

[19] The text of the epitaph has been recorded by several scholars, resulting in several variant readings. Unfortunately, the monument has been broken and further weathered over time, making the reconciliation of these contradictory readings impossible. Some editors have doubted even that this is a Christian dedication.

[20] Sheppard ("Jews, Christians, and Heretics," 179) sees the numerological reference as a sign of Jewish influence, and Louis Robert, *Hellenica* 11-12 (Paris: Maisonneuve, 1960) 419, noted that the name of the holy man, Roubes (who is buried with Gaios) is a Greek translation of the Jewish name, Reuben. However, because the Christian epitaphs contain a number of elements which are paralleled in Greek magical texts, the numerological influence need not be specifically Jewish. Robert Allison helped me to understand the meaning of these lines.

[21] The "angel of Roubes" appears in no. 4.13 following as guardian of a tomb.

μηδεὶς δ᾽ ἐν πλούτῳ τυφ[ω]– / θεὶς [γα]ῦρα [φ]ρονείτω· /
πᾶσι γὰρ εἷς ῞Αδης καὶ τέ– / λος ἐστὶν ἴσον. /
16 ἔστιν τις μέγας ὢν ἐν κτή– / μασιν; οὐ πλέον οὗτος /
ταὐτὸ μέτρον γαίης πρὸς / τάφον ἐκδέχεται. /
σπεύδετε, τὴν ψυχὴν / εὐ[φ]ραίνετε πάντοτε, θνη[τοί], /
[ὡ]ς ἡδὺς βίοτος καὶ μέτρο[ν] / ἐστὶ ζοῆς. /
20 ταῦτα [φ]ίλοι· μετὰ ταῦτα τί / γὰρ πλέον; οὐκέτι
ταῦτα· / στήλλη ταῦτα λαλεῖ καὶ λί– / θος. οὐ γὰρ
ἐγώ. /

Θύραι μὲν ἔνθα κα[ὶ] / πρὸς ᾿Αίδαν ὁδοὶ, /
24 ἀνεξόδευτοι δ᾽ εἰσ[ὶν] / ἐς φάος τρίβοι· /
οἱ δὴ δίκαιοι πάντο[τ᾽] / εἰς ἀνάστασιν /
[πρ]οδε[ικνύ]ουσι. το[ῦ]– / το δυνά[στης ?] Θεὸς /
(...3 lines illegible) / ....ποιμ[ένα]– /
28 το.......... / ἀ[νάστα]σις.

On the other hand, no one deluded by wealth should dare to exult;
for there is one Hades and an equal end (awaiting us) all.
Is someone great in possessions? He receives for a tomb no more
than this same measure of earth.
Hurry mortals! Gladden (your) soul(s) at all times,
for a sweet way of living also is the measure of life.
So friends, after this, what more is there? Nothing more.[22]
A stele of stone babbles these things, not I.

There are the doors and the path to Hades,
but there is no way out to the light.
The righteous, then, always show the way to resurrection.
This, the Lord God...........

Publication: Sheppard, "Jews, Christians, and Heretics," 176ff; Louis
Robert, *Hellenica* 11-12 (Paris: Maisonneuve 1960) 414ff.

---

[22] There seems to be real tension between such traditional-sounding sentiments
and the reference to "resurrection" following. One would like to know if the tension
existed in the mind of Gaios, or whether it is perhaps a mirage created by the
continued use of conventional formulaic expressions in the epitaphs.

(4.13) Marble bomos from Eski Haydan/Eumeneia.

Ἔτι ζῶντος
Λυκίδας μάρ–
τυρα τὸν
4 Θεὸν δίδω
ὅτι κατεσ–
κεύασα τὸ ἡ–
ρῷον, νω–
8 θρῶς ἔχον–
τος Ἀμιανοῦ
τοῦ ἀδεαφοῦ
μου, ἀπὸ τῶν
12 ἐμῶν καμάτων
καὶ ἐντέλλομε
Φρονίμη\<ν\> καὶ Μά–
ξιμαν τὰς ἀδελ–
16 φάς μου τεθῆνε
μφνας· εἴ τις δὲ
ἕτερον θήσει, ἔσ–
τε αὐτῷ πρὸς
20 τὸν Θεὸν καὶ
τὸν ἄνγελον
τὸν Ρουβῆ–
δος.

10. ἀδεαφοῦ = ἀδελφοῦ

17. μφνας = μόνας

(4.13) Marble bomos from Eski Haydan/Eumeneia.

> I, Lykidas,
>
> while still living,
>
> give God
>
> as my witness
>
> that I constructed
>
> this shrine
>
> out of (the proceeds of)
>
> my own labors (alone),
>
> due to the
>
> laziness of my
>
> brother, Amianos, and
>
> I authorize
>
> only my sisters,
>
> Phronima and
>
> Maxima,
>
> to be placed (in it).
>
> If anyone
>
> should inter
>
> another (corpse besides these two),
>
> he will reckon
>
> with God
>
> and the angel
>
> of Roubes.

Publication: Sheppard, "Jews, Christians, and Heretics," 175–76; Louis Robert, *Hellenica* 11-12 (Paris: Maisonneuve, 1960) 429ff.

(4.14) Bomos from Emircik/Eumeneia.

(A)Ἰ ῎Ε]τους τλα΄ μ(ηνὸς) β΄,
Αὐρ(ήλιος) ᾽Αλέξανδρος
Τηίου φ(υλῆς) ᾽Απολλων–
4 [ί]δος καὶ Αὐρ(ηλία) Ζηνω–
νὶς ἡ γυνὴ αὐτοῦ κα–
τεσκεύασαν τὸ ἡρῷ–
ον ἑαυτοῖς καὶ τοῖς
8 τέκνοις αὐτῶν ᾽Αμμ–
ιᾳ καὶ Μεσσαλείνῃ καὶ
Ζηνωνίδι καὶ ᾽Αλε–
ξανδρείᾳ ἤ ἂν ἄτε–
12 κνος ἐξ αὐτῶν τελε[υ]–
τήσῃ· εἰ δέ τις ἕτερον ἐπε–
νένκῃ πτῶμα ἔστα[ι]
[α]ὐτῷ πρὸς τὸν Θε–
16 ὸν καὶ νῦν καὶ τῷ π–
[α]ντὶ αἰῶνι καὶ μὴ τύ–
[χ]υτο τῆς τοῦ Θεοῦ [ἐ]–
πανγελίας, καὶ ὃς [ἂν]
20 [κ]ωλύσει αὐτῶν [τεθῆ]–
ναι τινα τῇ προ[κιμέ]–
[νῃ] αἱρέσι ἐ[νέχοιτο].

(4.14) Bomos from Emircik/Eumeneia.

> (A) (In the) year 331 (Sullan Era= C.E. 246),
>   second month, Aurelios Alexandros,
>   the son of Teios, (residing in) the Phyle
>   of Apollon (in Eumeneia), and Aurelia Zenonis,
>   his wife, constructed
>   this shrine for themselves
>   and for their children: Ammia
>   and Messaleina and
>   Zenonis and
>   Alexandreia — should any
>   of them die childless.[23]
>   If anyone should insert
>   another corpse (here),
>   he will reckon with God
>   both now and for all
>   eternity and not
>   obtain the promise of God;[24] and may
>   he who should prevent any of those (authorized)
>   from being interred
>   (here) suffer the
>   aforementioned condition (also).

---

[23] The significance of this stipulation is unclear. "Childless" could perhaps mean "unmarried", there could be a problem with available space, or maybe childbirth was viewed as a crucial experience which transferred a woman from one family to another.

[24] The "promise" presumably is "salvation" /resurrection.

(B) Αὐρ(ήλιος) Ζωτικὸς Γαὶ-
24 ου κατεσκεύασεν τὸ
ἡρῷον τὸ ἀπὸ βορέ-
ου ἑαυτῷ καὶ τῇ γυ-
νεκὶ αὐτοῦ Αυρ(ηλία) Κό-
28 μψῃ· μετὰ δὲ αὐτού[ς]
κηδευθῆναι οὐδε-
νὶ ἑτέρῳ ἐξὸν ἔ<σ>ται θ[εῖ]-
ναι ἰς αὐτὸ εἰ μὴ τιν-
32 α αὐτοὶ θέλουσιν
ἰς αὐτὸ κηδεῦσα[ί]
τινα μέχρι ζῶσιν· με-
τὰ δὲ ταῦτα εἴ τις ἔτε-
36 ρον ἐπιχείρησει θεῖνα[ι]
ἔσ<ται> αὐτῷ πρὸς τὸν Θε-
ὸν καὶ μὴ τύχυτο τ-
[ῆς] τοῦ Θεοῦ ἐπανγ[ε]-
40 [λίας............]

(B) Aurelios Zotikos, the son of
Gaios, constructed the
shrine on the north side
for himself and for
his wife, Aurelia
Kompse. After they are
interred, no other (corpse) is to be put
into it except
any which they authorized
to be interred in it
while (themselves) still living.
Thereafter,
if anyone tries
to insert another,
he will reckon with
God and not obtain
the promise of God.........

Publication: Calder, "Early-Christian Epitaphs," *AS* 5 (1955) 38.

(4.15) Stele from Ahmed-Serai/vicinity of Laodikea (Pontica).

Τὸν πάσης σοφίης καὶ ἀ-
ρετῆς κεκοσμημένον
ἄνδρα ῾Ρῆγλον ἅμα
4 δυεῖν τέκνοις ἐνθά-
δε γαῖ᾽ ἀμφεκάλυψε·
οὐνόματα δὲ τεκέ-
ων ᾽Ολυμπί<ο>ν ᾽Ακυλῖνα
8 τ<ε>, ὧν Θεὸς γενέτης ψυ-
[χ]ὰς αὐτὸς ἀντελάβετ[ο]
[με]μνημένος εὐσεβίης [ἣν]
[εἰ]ργάσαντο κατὰ κόσμ[ον]·
12 ἀνθ᾽ ὧν πτωχοὺς ἐν[έ]πλησα[ν]
ἀγαθῶν φίλους τ᾽ ἐτίμη-
σαν, στοργῇ δὲ πολλῇ καὶ ἀ-
μιμήτῳ συμγενείην ἐφύλα-
16 ξαν καὶ πᾶσι βροτοῖς φιλο-
ξενίην ἀσμένως ἐπό-
θησαν. τὸν ποθινόν καὶ
ἀσύμκριτον σύμβιον ἅμα
20 τοῖς γλυκυτάτοις τέκνοις
ἐλεινὴ ᾽Ακυλλία μνημονεύω·
τὸν προσκυνητὸν πατέρα [ἅμ]-
[α γ]λυκυτάτοις ἀδελφ[οῖς...]
24 [...] καὶ ᾽Ακυλῖνος μ[νημονεύ ?]-
[ομεν· τὸ]ν ἐν πᾶσιν εὔ[στορ]-
[γο]ν καὶ [γ]νή[σ]ιον φίλον ᾽Ιο[υλι]-
ανὸς μνημονεύω.

(4.15) Stele from Ahmed-Serai/vicinity of Laodikea (Pontica).

> Here Earth enshrouded the man, Reglos,
> who has been adorned with all wisdom and virtue,
> together with his two children. The names of
> the children are Olympion and Akylina,
> whose spirits God the Begetter[25]
> himself received, remembering the piety
> (of their) deeds in the world,
> in reward for the fact that they filled beggars
> with good things; and they honored their friends,
> they watched over their family with great
> and inimitable affection, and they were readily
> anxious to be hospitable to all men.
> I, unhappy Akyllia, commemorate my longed-for
> and incomparable husband, together with my dearest
> children. We, (_____) and Akylinos, commemorate
> our honored father together with our dearest
> brother and sister. I, Ioulianos (?),
> commemorate my friend-- in every way
> a beloved and noble man.

Publication: J.G.C. Anderson, F. Cumont, and H. Gregoire, *Studia Pontica* 3 (Brussels: Lamertin, 1910) no. 20.

---

[25]Θεὸς γενέτης. Lacking any reference to Jesus/Christ/Son, this God who receives the spirits of the right-living may not be specifically the senior element of the Trinity. The description of piety which follows, however, seemed to the original editors of the text likely to reflect Christianity.

(4.16) Marble stele from Kütahya Museum (provenance unknown).

Αὐρ(ήλιος) Ἀθηνόδοτος Δοκιμεὺς τεχνίτης ἐποίησε
τὸ ἔργον.
Ἔνθα χθὼν κατέχι Ἀκάκιον σώ-
φροναν ἄνδρα, Μηνοδώρου υἱόν, θεοτίμητον ἀληθῶς,
4 ἥσιον ἐν κόσμῳ ἑῆς πάτρης κα-
τὰ πάντα· τριάκοντα ἔτη ἐν
χηροσύνῃ ὑπομίνας, μουνό-
γαμος μοῦνον τεῦξεν τέκνον ἐν βιό-
8 τοιο, τοὔνομα Λουκίλλαν τὴν σώφρο-
να, τῷ πατρὶ κῦδος· δῶκεν δ' αὐτὴν ἀνδρὶ ἐφ' ἐλπίσι γηροκομηθην ἀνεψιῷ
Τροφίμῳ· τύχαν δὲ κακῶν ὑμενέων,
12 ὄκτω κὲ δέκα μῆνας μεθ' αὐτὸν οὐκ
ἐβίωσεν· πικραὶ γὰρ Μοῖραι ἴσους μίτους
ἐπέκλωσαν μητρὶ κὲ θυγατρὶ ὅμοια Πρω-
τεσιλάου. Δόμνη σεμνοτάτη τύμβοις
16 ἰδίοισι δὲ κῖται. τριάκοντα ἔτη θυγατέ-

1. Δοκιμεὺς τεχνίτης. As the site of Phrygia's major marble quarry, Dokimeion was home to a substantial population of stoneworkers. For further information, see J. Clayton Fant, *Cavum Antrum Phrygiae: The Organization and Operations of the Roman Imperial Marble Quarries in Phrygia* (Oxford: B.A.R. International Series 482, 1989).

10. γηροκομηθην = γηροκομηθῆναι. Calder, "Early Christian Epitaphs," 32: "I have left γηροκομηθην, which scans and is therefore deliberate, without accent..."

(4.16) Marble stele from Kütahya Museum (provenance unknown).

Aurelios Athenodotos, a (stone)craftsman from Dokimeion
made this work.

In this ground lies Akakios, the son of Menodoros,
a temperate man, truly blessed by God,
lucky above all in the behavior of his family.
Thirty years he lived as a widower.
Married only once, he sired one child during (his) life,
(a daughter) named Loukilla, a chaste girl,
an honor to her father.
He gave her to a husband, (her?) cousin, Trophimos,
hoping for support in (his) old age.
By chance, their wedding was unlucky.
She lived less than eighteen months beside him.
For the bitter fates spun an equal thread (of life)
for (both) mother and daughter,
(short threads) like (that of) Protesilaos.[26]
Domne, most respected (mother), rests in a
tomb of her own. At the age of thirty,

---

[26] Calder, "Early Christian Epitaphs," 32: "...fourth-century Christians often seek an opportunity to show that they know their Homer."

ραν κατέλιψε, τεσσαρέτη πάλιν αὐτὴ τὸν
πατέραν ἐπρόαξεν· τύμβοις παππώοις
μετὰ τοῦ πατρὸς ἐνθάδε κῖτη. ἄνδρες
20 πρεσβύτατοι κὲ ὁμήλικες ἠδὲ νέοι τε,
δῆριν πρὸς τίναν ἔσχον; οὐ πρὸς νέον οὐδὲ
γέροντα· τιμῇ τῇ μεγάλῃ παρὰ πάτρης πα–
ρεπέμφθην· Θεός πού μ᾽ ἐκέλευσ᾽· ἐνὴ Πλου–
24 τεῖ ἢ Παραδίζῳ μίσθους ἀντιλάβοιτε παρ᾽ ἀθανάτου
Θεοῦ / αὐτοῦ· ἐμοὶ γὰρ οὐ μελέτη· κακὸν κόσμον
κατέλιψα. / τὴν σφραγῖδα Θεὸς ἐμοὶ τέκνῳ διασώζι·
θνητὸς ἐν ἀθανά–/ τοις Ἀβρα[μ κ]όλποις τετύχηκα,
28 Θεῷ δουλεύω, Παραδιζοισι / κατοικῶ.

27. Ἀβρα[μ κ]όλποις. Calder, "Early Christian Epitaphs," 33, note 2: "In the gap ... there is barely room for two letters ... Cf. Ἀβραμίοις κόλποις in MAMA 7, no. 587 = MAMA 1, p. xxvi." Cf. also Luke 16:23 and Augustine, *Confessions* 9.3 (referring to the death of a friend): *et nunc ille vivit in sinu Abraham.*

she left behind (her) daughter (Loukilla),

who herself predeceased (her) father by

four years. She lies here with her father

in the ancestral tomb.

Elders, comrades, and youths-- have I fought

against anyone? Not (indeed) against the young

nor against the old. I was escorted (to my grave ?)

with great honor by my family. Perhaps God commanded

me. May you claim (your due) wages in Hades or Paradise

from immortal God himself. For to me it matters not.

I leave behind an evil world.

God preserves the Seal for me, (his) child.[27]

I, a mortal, have landed in the immortal lap

of Abraham. I am a servant of God.

I live in Paradise.

Publication: Calder, "Early-Christian Epitaphs," 31ff, no. 1.

---

[27] Cf. the reference to "an illustrious Seal" in no. 2.15. These conventionally have been interpreted as references to the "Seal" of baptism. Calder, "Early Christian Epitaphs," 32–33, classifies this as a Christian monument because of this reference, the use of the 'significant' Christian name, Akakios, and the geneal moral tone of the epitaph.

(4.17) Stele from Iznik/Nikaea.

    Αὐρηλία Χρήστη
    Πωλίωνος Αὐρηλίῳ
    ᾽Αττικῷ καὶ Αὐρηλίᾳ
4   Τροφιμίᾳ καὶ ἐμαυτῇ
    τὸ μνημεῖον κατεσκεύ–
    ασα ἐπὶ τῷ μετὰ τὸ κα–
    τατεθῆναι ἡμᾶς ἀμφο–
8   τέρους εἶναι αὐτὸ ἄ–
    σκυλτον, εἰ μὴ τέκνον
    ἡμῶν τι πάθη· εἰ δὲ τις
    ἕτερος σκύλῃ, δώσει λό–
12 γον τῷ Θεῷ ἐν ἡμερᾳ κρίσ[εως].

(4.18) Sarcophagus from Korase ?/territory of Philomelion.

    [– – – – – – – –]
    [– – –] ὃς <δὲ> ἂν ταύτη τ[ῇ]
    σορ[ῷ] κακοεργέα
    χεῖρα
4   προσοίσει, δώσ–
    ει τῷ Θεῷ λόγον
    τῷ μέλλοντι κρεί–
    νειν ζῶ[ν]τας κὲ
8   νεκρούς.

(4.17) Stele from Iznik/Nikaea.

> I, Aurelia Chreste,
>
> daughter of Polion,
>
> constructed this monument
>
> for Aurelios Attikos, Aurelia Trophimia,
>
> and myself, on the condition that
>
> after we are interred together
>
> it is to be inviolable unless
>
> a child of ours should die.
>
> If any other should violate it,
>
> he will give account to God
>
> on Judgment Day.[28]

Publication: Şahin, *Iznik* 1, no. 556; G. Mendel, "Inscriptions de Bithynie," *BCH* 24 (1900) 389, no. 45.

(4.18) Sarcophagus from Korase ?/territory of Philomelion.

> ....
>
> ..whoever should lay evil-doing hands
>
> on this sarcophagus will give account
>
> to God who will judge the living
>
> and the dead.

Publication: W.M. Ramsay, "The Cities and Bishoprics of Phrygia," *Journal of Hellenic Studies* 4 (1883) 434, no. 43.

---

[28] Cf. the (probably) Jewish dedications which refer to Judgment: nos. 1.20 and 1.22.

(4.19) Stele from Silivri/Selymbria.

✝ Ἐνθάδε κατάκι–
τε Σώζον πρεσβύ–
τερος Χριστιανὸς
4 χορίου Νητουμε–
γάλης ὑπὸ Νακο–
λίαν, μη(νὸς) πένπτο<υ> ἐν–
άτῃ, ἐνδ(ικτιῶνος) ιε΄ · ἔχι πρὸς
8 τὸ[ν Θεόν– – –].

(4.19) Stele from Silivri/Selymbria.

> ✝ Here lies the Christian
>
> presbyter, Sozon,
>
> of the village of Greater Netos,
>
> in the territory of Nakoleia,
>
> (who died on) the ninth (day)
>
> of the fifth month in indiction fifteen.
>
> He must reckon with [God].[29]

Publication: Louis Robert, *A travers l'Asie mineure* (Bibliothèque des Écoles Françaises d'Athènes et de Rome 239; Paris: de Boccard, 1980) 309.

---

[29] The familiar curse formula appears in this late (perhaps fifth century) epitaph without reference to any violator, and may here describe an individual reckoning of the deceased with God.

INDICES

(A) PERSONAL NAMES

Aurelios Alexandros 3 (no. 4.14)
Aurelios Amianos (no. 1.11)
Aurelios Antiochos (no. 2.20)
Aurelios Artemas (no. 3.18)
Aurelios Athenodotos (no. 4.16)
Aurelios Attikos (no. 4.17)
Aurelios Charidemos (no. 3.8)
Aurelios Chrestos (no. 3.15)
Aurelios Chrysanthos (no. 2.20)
Aurelios Chrysogonos (no. 1.16)
Aurelios Dionoisios (no. 2.14)
Aurelios Dionysios (no. 2.12)
Aurelios Eirenaios (no. 1.11)
Aurelios Eistratonikos (no. 2.5)
Aurelios Eutyches Helix (no. 3.4)
Aurelios Eutychos 1 (no. 2.11)
Aurelios Eutychos 2 (no. 2.11)
Aurelios Glykon (no. 1.10)
Aurelios Kyrion (no. 1.22)
Aurelios Mannos (no. 3.9)
Aurelios Markellos (no. 2.8)
Aurelios Meiros (no. 3.11)
Aurelios Menedemos (no. 1.9)
Aurelios Messalas (no. 3.6)
Aurelios Neikeros (no. 3.9)
Aurelios Ouales (no. 2.19)
Aurelios Panmeneos (no. 1.11)
Aurelios Papas (no. 2.9)
Aurelios Patrikis (Plate)
Aurelios Phrougianos (no. 1.23)
Aurelios Romulos (no. 3.10)
Aurelios Senekianos (no. 3.10)
Aurelios Spoudasis (no. 3.17)
Aurelios Zotikos 1 (no. 1.24)
Aurelios Zotikos 2 (no. 3.3)
Aurelios Zotikos 3 (no. 3.3)
Aurelios Zotikos 4 (no. 4.14)
Aurelios Zotikos Markianos (no. 2.3)
Aurila Mama (no. 3.11)

Baleria (no. 2.20)

Chreste (no.1.8)
Chrysippos (no. 3.1)
Chrysogonos 1 (no. 1.12)
Chrysogonos 2 (no. 1.15)

Deios 1 (no. 1.3)
Deios 2 (no. 1.3)
Demetrianos (no. 3.1)
Diogas (no. 4.8)
Diogenes 1 (no. 2.8)
Diogenes 2 (no. 3.5)
Dionysas (no. 2.5)
Dionysios (no. 3.3)
Domitios Heliodoros (no. 3.1)
Domna 1 (Plate)
Domna 2 (no. 2.4)
Domna 3 (no. 2.7)
Domna 4 (no. 2.7)
Domna 5 (no. 2.11)
Domne (no. 4.16)

Eistratonikos (no. 2.5)
Eleutheros (no. 1.12)
Epaphrodeitos (no. 1.12)
Epigonos (no. 3.2)
Epiktes (Plate)
Erpidephoros (no. 2.5)
Eugenios (no. 4.10)
Eukarpie (no. 3.8)
Eumoirios Papos (no. 3.14)
Euphemia (no.4.1)
Euphemos (no. 2.16)
Eutyches 1 (no. 2.2)
Eutyches 2 (no. 2.2)
Eutychianes (no. 2.11)
Eutychion (1.12)

Flabia Sosanne (no. 3.7)
Flabios Nikias (no. 3.16)
Flaouia Diogenia (no. 3.12)
Flaouia Ioulia Flaouiane (no. 3.5)

INDICES

Paulos 2 (no. 2.15)
Paulos 3 (no. 4.3)
Paulos 4 (no. 4.11)
Pausanios (no. 1.2)
Phellinas (no. 2.2)
Philetos (no. 2.5)
Philippos (no. 2.17)
Phronima (no. 4.13)
Polion (no.4.17)
Praxios (no. 3.3)
Prokla 1 (no. 2.11)
Prokla 2 (no. 2.11)
Protesilaos (no. 4.16)

Reglos (no. 4.15)
Roubes (nos. 4.12- 4.13)
Sanbatios (no. 3.12)
Seuerianos (no. 1.15)
Sextilios (no. 1.10)
Sophronie (no. 3.7)
Sosthas (no. 2.7)
Sosthenes (no. 2.7)
Sostrate (no. 1.13)
Sozon (no. 4.19)

Tatia 1 (no. 2.2)
Tatia 2 (no. 3.18)
Tatia 3 (no. 4.12)
Tation (no. 3.2)
Teios (no. 4.14)
Telesphoros (no. 2.6)
Thalamos (no. 1.8)
Thallos (no. 1.6)
Tieos (no. 3.11)
Trophima (no. 2.18)
Trophimos 1 (no.4.2)
Trophimos 2 (no. 4.7)
Trophimos 3 (no. 4.16)

Zenodotos (no. 3.13)
Zenonis (no. 4.14)
Zoe (no. 1.6)

Zotikos 1 (Plate)
Zotikos 2 (no. 2.6)

(B) PLACE NAMES

Arados (Phoenicia) (no. 3.14)
Asia (no. 4.10)

Dokimeion (no. 4.16)

Eumeneia (nos. 1.24, 3.2, 3.3, 3.4)
Euphrates (no. 2.15)

Greater Netos (no. 4.19)

Herakleia (Thrace) (no. 2.8)
Hieropolis (nos. 2.13, 2.15)

Kouessos (no. 3.5)

Laodikea (Katakekaumene) (no. 3.5)

Nakoleia (no. 4.19)
Nikaea (no. 3.17)
Nisibis (no. 2.15)

Phrygia (no. 4.10)
Pisidia (no. 3.5)
Puteolis (no. 1.3)

Rome (no. 2.15)

Sebaste (no. 3.6)
Soumna (no. 2.9)
Syria (no. 2.15)

Tarsus (no. 1.6)
Temenothyrai (no. 2.2)

(C) RELIGION (NON-CHRISTIAN)

Apollon Archegetos (Semiaphoroi
   of) (no. 1.14)
Deuteronomy (no. 1.23)
Herakles (no. 1.6)
Jew (no. 1.20)
katachthonic gods (nos. 1.13, 1.17)
synagogue (no. 1.20)
synagogue of the Jews (no. 1.21)
theos/god (traditional) (no. 1.1)
Theos/God (Jewish) (nos. 1.22,
   1.24=Name of God)
Zeus (no.1.18)
Zeus Bronton (no. 1.12)
Zeus Solymos (nos. 1.15, 1.16)

(D) RELIGION (CHRISTIAN)

Abraham (no. 4.16)
angel (of Roubes) (no. 4.13)
bishop (nos. 3.5, 4.8)
Christian(s) (nos. 2.1, 2.2, 3.5,
   4.19)
Christians for Christians (Plate;
   nos. 2.3, 2.4, 2.5, 2.6, 2.7,
   2.11)
church (no. 3.5)
continence (life of) (no. 4.6)
First Angel (no. 4.10)
Hades (nos. 4.12, 4.16)
Holy Church of God of the
   Novatians (no. 4.9)
Holy Church of God of the Pure
   Ones (no. 4.10)
Holy Shepherd (nos. 2.13, 2.15)
Holy Virgin (no. 2.15)
Judgment Day (nos. 2.20, 4.17,
   4.18)
koinonos (no. 4.7)

Lord (no. 4.1)
martyr (nos. 4.2, 4.3, 4.4, 4.7)
moistes= mystes (no. 4.7)
Paradise (no.4.16)
Paul (no. 2.15)
presbyter (nos. 2.7, 2.14, 4.5, 4.8,
   4.9, 4.10, 4.19)
reader (no. 4.1)
resurrection (no. 4.12)
Seal (nos. 2.15, 4.16)
Theos/God (nos. 2.2, 2.16, 2.18,
   2.19, 2.20, 3.1, 3.2, 3.3, 3.6,
   3.7, 3.8, 3.9, 3.10, 3.11, 3.12,
   3.13, 4.1, 4.2, 4.5, 4.7,
   4.10,4.13, 4.14, 4.16, 4.17,
   4.18, 4.19)
   Almighty God (no. 3.5)
   Deathless/Immortal God (nos.
     3.18, 4.16)
   God the Begetter (no. 4.15)
   Great God (no. 4.12)
   Living God (nos. 2.17, 3.4)
   Lord God (no. 4.12)
Trinity (no. 4.11)
virgins (no. 4.5)

(E) GOVERNMENT (CIVIL AND IMPERIAL)

administrator (no. 3.1)
agonothete (no. 3.1)
agoranomos (no. 1.23)
archives (no. 1.11)
archon (no. 3.1)
armorer (no. 3.11)
boule (nos. 1.24, 3.2, 3.3, 3.4,
   3.5, 3.6, 3.7)
Caesars (no. 1.8)
campidoctorum (no. 4.11)
chreophylakeion (no. 2.10)
fiscus (nos. 1.9, 1.11, 1.14, 3.3)

1.22, 1.23, 1.24, 2.7, 2.8,
2.16, 2.17, 2.18, 2.19, 2.20,
3.2, 3.3, 3.4, 3.6, 3.7, 3.8,
3.9, 3.10, 3.11, 3.12, 3.13,
3.18, 4.1, 4.2, 4.5, 4.13, 4.14,
4.17, 4.18)

Funereary fines (nos. 1.9, 1.11,
1.14, 1.15, 1.16, 1.20, 1.21,
1.24, 2.13, 2.15, 3.3)

(I) KINSHIP/RELATIONSHIP
TERMS

ἀδελφή (Plate, nos. 1.16, 2.18,
4.5, 4.13)
ἀδελφός (nos. 1.24, 2.1, 2.3, 2.11,
2.14, 3.1, 4.6, 4.13, 4.15)
ἄλοχος (no. 4.12)
ἀνήρ (nos. 2.1, 2.4, 2.5, 2.17,
3.16, 4.11)
ἀνεψιός (no. 4.16)
γαμβρός (nos. 2.6, 2.7, 3.1)
γένος (no. 3.5)
γονεύς (nos. 1.11, 2.3, 2.7)
γυναικάδελφος (no. 3.10)
γυνή (1.11, 1.16, 1.23, 1.24, 2.1,
2.2, 2.7, 2.8, 3.2, 3.3, 3.4,
3.8, 3.9, 3.11, 3.13, 3.15,
3.18, 4.14)
ἐγγόνη (no. 2.7)
ἔγγονος (nos. 2.6, 2.11, 2.20)
ἔκγονος (no. 3.6)
ἑκυρός (no. 2.4)
ἐνάτηρ (no.2.11)
θεῖος (no. 3.1)
θεία (no. 4.6)
θρεπτή (no. 3.7)
θυγάτηρ (nos. 1.5, 1.23, 2.7, 3.1,
3.3, 3.5, 4.16)
κηδεστρία (no. 3.10)

μήτηρ (Plate, nos. 1.5, 1.10,
1.12, 1.23, 2.4, 2.12, 3.1,
4.16)
νύμφη (nos. 2.4, 2.11)
παιδίον (no. 2.1)
πατήρ (Plate, nos. 1.10, 1.12,
1.15 2.2, 2.5, 2.12, 4.9, 4.15,
4.16)
πενθερός (nos. 2.7, 2.20)
σύμβιος (nos. 1.9, 1.13, 1.14,
1.15, 1.22, 2.6, 2.7, 2.9, 2.20,
3.6, 3.7, 3.10, 3.17, 4.15)
σύζυγος (no. 2.19)
σύντεκνος (no. 2.7)
τηθίς (no. 3.3)
τέκνον (nos. 1.1, 1.11, 1.22, 2.4,
2.5, 2.7, 2.8, 2.9, 2.11, 2.17,
3.3, 3.4, 3.8, 3.9, 3.13, 3.15,
3.18, 4.14, 4.15, 4.16, 4.17)
τέκος (no. 4.12)
τεκοῦσα (no. 1.20)
υἱός (Plate, nos. 1.9, 2.16, 3.3,
3.10, 3.11, 3.12, 4.4)

CPSIA information can be obtained at www.ICGtesting.com
Printed in the USA
LVOW040220070612

284914LV00002B/194/A